3?

ULTIMATE
GUIDE
TO THE
PREMIER
LEAGUE

Written by James Bandy
Image sourcing by Angus Reid
Designed by Daniel Brawn & Adam Wilsher

PBR

A Pillar Box Red Publication

A Pillar Box Red Publication

© 2018. Published by Pillar Box Red Publishing Limited. Printed in the EU.

ISBN: 978-1-912456-19-2

CONTENTS

132-188

Season-By-Season Reviews

CONTENTS

THE HISTORY OF THE PREMIER LEAGUE

The Premier League is the most-watched sports league in the world, broadcast in 212 territories to 643 million homes, with a potential TV audience of 4.7 billion people.

But it wasn't always this way. Despite significant European success in the 1970s and early 1980s, the late 1980s marked a low point for English football. Stadiums were crumbling, supporters had to put up with poor facilities, hooliganism was rife, and English clubs were banned from European competitions for five years following the Heysel Stadium disaster in 1985.

The Football League First Division, the top level of English football since 1888, was behind leagues such as Italy's Serie A and Spain's La Liga in attendances and revenues, and several top English players had moved abroad.

By the turn of the 1990s the downward trend was starting to reverse. At the 1990 FIFA World Cup, England reached the semi-finals. UEFA, European football's governing body, lifted the five-year ban on English clubs playing in European competitions in 1990 and Man. United lifted the UEFA Cup Winners' Cup the following year. The Taylor Report on stadium safety standards, which proposed expensive upgrades to create all-seater stadiums in the aftermath of the Hillsborough disaster, was published in January of that year.

In 1990, the managing director of London Weekend Television, Greg Dyke, met with the representatives of the 'Big Five' football clubs in England (Manchester United, Liverpool, Tottenham, Everton and Arsenal). The meeting was to pave the way for a break away from The Football League. The five clubs decided it was a good idea and decided to press ahead with it.

At the close of the 1991 season, a proposal was made for the establishment of a new league that would bring more money into the game overall. The Founder Members Agreement, signed on 17 July 1991 by the game's top-flight clubs, established the basic principles for setting up the FA Premier League. In 1992, the First Division clubs resigned from the Football League en masse and on 27 May, 1992 the FA Premier League was formed.

The league held its first season in 1992-93 and was made up of 22 clubs. The 22 inaugural members of the new Premier League were: Arsenal, Aston Villa, Blackburn Rovers, Chelsea, Coventry City, Crystal Palace, Everton, Ipswich Town, Leeds United, Liverpool, Manchester City, Manchester United, Middlesbrough, Norwich City, Nottingham Forest, Oldham Athletic, Queens Park Rangers, Sheffield United, Sheffield Wednesday, Southampton, Tottenham Hotspur, and Wimbledon. Luton Town, Notts County, and West Ham United were the three teams relegated from the old First Division at the end of the 1991–92 season and didn't take part in the inaugural Premier League season.

Since then, the Premier League has gone from strength to strength. As well as attracting the best players from all over the world, the League can now boast many of the top managers too. Fantastic new stadiums have been built or existing

ones have been updated, attendances have soared, and the drama, tension and excitement seem to increase every year.

From Man. United's dominance in the early years to Jack Walker's Blackburn shocking the football world in 1995, from Arsenal's 'Invincibles' of 2003-04 to Jose Mourinho arriving at Chelsea as 'The Special One'. From Kevin Keegan's Newcastle nearly-men to Alex Ferguson's brilliance, from Leicester's incredible 5000/1 Premier League win to Man. City's record-breaking team of 2017-18, the Premier League has a rich and compelling history.

With legendary players, managers, matches and goals having graced the Premier League, it's been an incredible first 26 years.

EVERY PREMIER LEAGUE CLUB REVEALED!

Since the Premier League began in 1992, it has featured 49 different teams. Some clubs, including Man. United, Arsenal and Everton, have played in the League every season since its inception, while others, like Blackpool, Swindon and Barnsley, have been one-season wonders. Below is a map of showing every club that has played in the competition up to the beginning of the 2018-19 campaign.

NEWCASTLE
24 SEASONS

SUNDERLAND
16 SEASONS

MIDDLESBROUGH
15 SEASONS

BURNLEY
5 SEASONS

BRADFORD
2 SEASONS

LEEDS
12 SEASONS

HUDDERSFIELD
2 SEASONS

BLACKPOOL
1 SEASON

BARNSLEY
1 SEASON

BLACKBURN
18 SEASONS

SHEFF. WED.
8 SEASONS

EVERTON
27 SEASONS

HULL
5 SEASONS

LIVERPOOL
27 SEASONS

NOTT'M FOREST
5 SEASONS

SHEFF. UTD.
3 SEASONS

LEICESTER
13 SEASONS

STOKE
10 SEASONS

SWANSEA
7 SEASONS

DERBY
7 SEASONS

NORWICH
8 SEASONS

CARDIFF
2 SEASONS

IPSWICH
5 SEASONS

SWINDON
1 SEASON

WATFORD
6 SEASONS

SOUTHAMPTON
20 SEASONS

BOURNEMOUTH
4 SEASONS

PORTSMOUTH
7 SEASONS

READING
3 SEASONS

BRIGHTON
2 SEASONS

GREATER MANCHESTER

BOLTON
13 SEASONS

WIGAN
8 SEASONS

OLDHAM
2 SEASONS

MAN. UNITED
27 SEASONS

MAN. CITY
22 SEASONS

WEST MIDLANDS

WOLVES
5 SEASONS

ASTON VILLA
24 SEASONS

WBA
12 SEASONS

BIRMINGHAM
7 SEASONS

COVENTRY
9 SEASONS

TOTTENHAM
27 SEASONS

ARSENAL
27 SEASONS

CHELSEA
27 SEASONS

WEST HAM
23 SEASONS

QPR
7 SEASONS

FULHAM
14 SEASONS

CHARLTON
8 SEASONS

LONDON

CRYSTAL PALACE
10 SEASONS

WIMBLEDON
8 SEASONS

15

THE 50 BEST PREMIER LEAGUE PLAYERS OF ALL TIME

It is a debate that has long raged, and will continue to do so evermore. The Premier League has changed dramatically since its first ever season in 1992-93, but so has football, the players and the requirements needed to succeed. It's difficult enough trying to compare and evaluate the thousands of players who have graced the League, but even more so when trying to compare players from different generations. When you try to compare the goalscorers with defensive titans, the midfield creators with the finest goalkeepers, and try to put a value on it, it's not easy. But it's definitely a debate worth having, so here are the 50 Best Premier League Players of All Time.

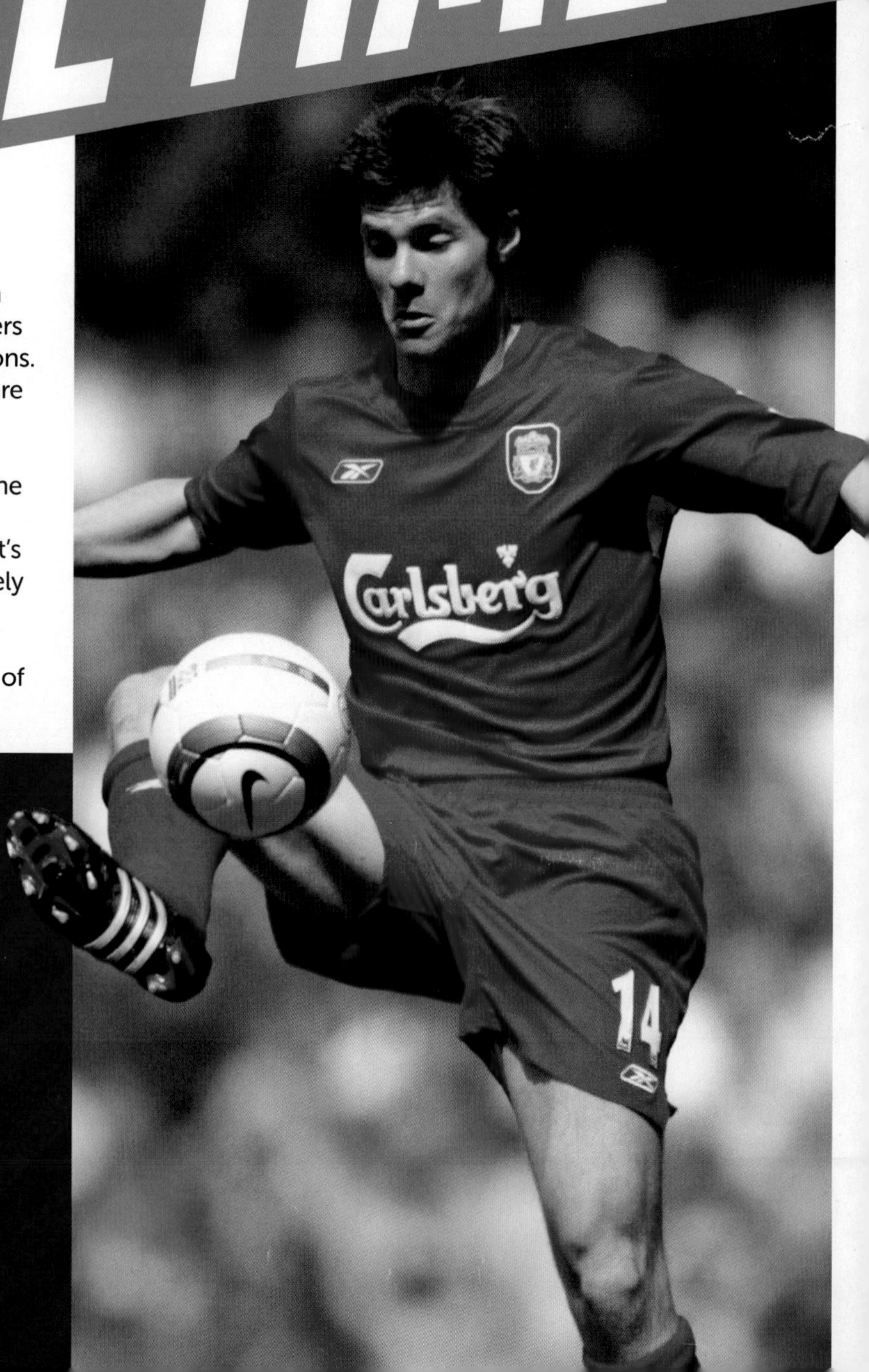

50 XABI ALONSO

PL Games: 143
PL Goals: 14
PL Assists: 17
PL Champion: 0
PL Clubs: Liverpool

Alonso's supreme passing ability and ice-cool awareness was vital in the Liverpool side that reached such heights for a few seasons under Rafa Benitez. It's no coincidence that both Steven Gerrard and Fernando Torres enjoyed their best form by far alongside the Basque playmaker, nor that the side fell off a cliff as soon as he left.

49
PAOLO DI CANIO
PL Games: 190
PL Goals: 66
PL Assists: 49
Pl Champion: 0
PL Clubs: Sheff. Wed., West Ham, Charlton
If you're able to separate the artist from his art, then it's impossible not to appreciate the sheer magnificence of Di Canio in his prime. The Italian could be temperamental, and at times downright crazy, but he also possessed one of the great right boots of the modern era, immortalised by the incredible kung-fu volley he sent flying past Neil Sullivan in March 2000.

48
EDWIN VAN DER SAR
PL Games: 313
PL Clean Sheets: 132
PL Assists: 1
PL Champion: 4
PL Clubs: Fulham, Man. United
A move to Fulham after two seasons at Juventus didn't seem like an obvious one, but during his four years in London he helped Fulham establish themselves in the top flight and proved himself to be one of the best keepers in the Premier League. Man. United snapped him up in 2005 and van der Sar went on to win four Premier League titles. Throw in a record 1,311 minutes without conceding a Premier League goal in 2009-10 and it's easy to see why the Dutchman is so highly regarded.

47
DENIS IRWIN
PL Games: 328
PL Goals: 18
PL Assists: 25
PL Champion: 7
PL Clubs: Man. United, Wolves
Denis Irwin hung up his boots in May 2004 after 22 years in the game, 12 of which had been in the Premier League with Man. United. During that time he won seven Premier League titles, and was one of the first names on Alex Ferguson's team-sheet. In an era of big characters at Old Trafford, Irwin went about his job with the minimum of fuss, and was probably hugely underestimated as a result of it.

46
ARJEN ROBBEN
PL Games: 67
PL Goals: 15
PL Assists: 16
PL Champion: 2
PL Clubs: Chelsea
Robben's career has soared to such heights since leaving England that it's easy to forget those first exciting glimpses of him as a young player at Chelsea. At times, he looked like the perfect Mourinho component: lightning-quick, direct and highly economic. He would become a better player at Real Madrid and Bayern Munich, but he was never more exciting to watch than he was between 2004 and 2007.

45
MICHAEL OWEN
PL Games: 326
PL Goals: 150
PL Assists: 31
PL Champion: 1
PL Clubs: Liverpool, Newcastle, Man. United, Stoke
Owen burst onto the Premier League scene as a 17-year-old in 1997, scoring on his Premier League debut and winning Premier League Golden Boots as a teenager. Between his debut and transfer to Real Madrid he was one of the best strikers around, with a pace and directness few defenders could handle. Injuries hampered his career but he had a spell at Newcastle before winning the Premier League with Man. United, ultimately ending his career at Stoke.

42
MARC OVERMARS
PL Games: 100
PL Goals: 25
PL Assists: 19
PL Champion: 1
PL Clubs: Arsenal
Overmars was only at Highbury for three seasons, but during that time made an impact that puts him up there with the best the Premier League has seen. Blessed with tremendous pace, quick feet and a decent finish, he won the Premier League and FA Cup double in his first season with the club. He joined Bar

44
GARY SPEED
PL Games: 535
PL Goals: 80
PL Assists: 44
PL Champion: 0
PL Clubs: Leeds, Everton, Newcastle, Bolton
Gary Speed made 535 Premier League appearances, a record at the time he retired, over the course of a career which spanned 22 years. He was the ultimate team player – while others grabbed the headlines, he would be the one most players would vote for as their Man of the Match each week. He had a knack of arriving in the penalty area at the right time to contribute vital goals, and an ability at the other end to read the game and cut out trouble. Quite simply, a brilliant professional.

43
DWIGHT YORKE
PL Games: 375
PL Goals: 123
PL Assists: 50
PL Champion: 3
PL Clubs: Aston Villa, Man. United, Blackburn, Birmingham, Sunderland
After joining Aston Villa in 1989 as a 17-year-old, Yorke burst onto the Premier League scene and wowed fans with his pace, tricks and finishing – and the fact he always played with a smile on his face. He moved to Man. United and formed a lethal partnership with Andy Cole, winning the Premier League three times, before Ruud van Nistelrooy's arrival at Old Trafford signalled his departure.

41
RUUD VAN NISTELROOY
PL Games: 150
PL Goals: 95
PL Assists: 14
PL Champion: 1
PL Clubs: Man. United
Man. United waited a full year to sign him from PSV due to a serious knee injury, but by the end of his five years at Old Trafford the club had been repaid in spades. The last great penalty-box striker, Van Nistelrooy only won one Premier League title, which hardly does his contribution justice. He hit a staggering 110 goals across his first three seasons at the club and interestingly, never scored from outside the box for the club.

40
ROBIN VAN PERSIE
PL Games: 280
PL Goals: 144
PL Assists: 53
PL Champion: 1
PL Clubs: Arsenal, Man. United

The 21-year-old Feyenoord forward arrived at Highbury in May 2004 but it was March 2011 that saw the start of a 14-month golden spell in which the striker barely stopped scoring. In August 2012, after netting 132 Arsenal goals, the Dutchman joined rivals Man. United in search of the Premier League Winner's Medal he craved. He was a revelation, winning the 2013 Golden Boot and the League title after grabbing 26 goals in 38 games.

39
JAMIE CARRAGHER
PL Games: 508
PL Goals: 3
PL Assists: 15
PL Champion: 0
PL Clubs: Liverpool

A tough, no-nonsense defender, Carragher made his Reds debut in 1997, scoring one of only three Premier League goals in that game. From that point he was a near ever-present in the side for the next 17 seasons, racking up 508 appearances. A born leader, he was loyal and brave, had great organisational ability and tactical awareness. He read the game superbly and would put his body on the line for the cause. A Reds legend.

38
LES FERDINAND
PL Games: 351
PL Goals: 149
PL Assists: 49
PL Champion: 0
PL Clubs: QPR, Newcastle, Tottenham, West Ham, Leicester, Bolton

Ferdinand scored 101 Premier League goals in his first five seasons, and was rightly feared by opposition defences everywhere he went. He could either play on the shoulder or the centre-back, often looking to get in behind the back line or spring an offside trap with a turn of pace, or using his upper-body strength to play with his back to goal. He also possessed a fearsome shot and had few equals in the air.

36
DAVID GINOLA

PL Games: 198
PL Goals: 21
PL Assists: 42
CL Champion: 0
PL Clubs: Newcastle, Tottenham, Aston Villa, Everton

When Ginola arrived at Newcastle from PSG in 1995 he was known as a maverick, but during the two seasons he was on Tyneside he was an integral part of Kevin Keegan's thrilling Newcastle side. The winger seemed to glide across the pitch, could beat defenders like they weren't there and had a sublime touch and mastery of the ball that saw him make some superb goals but make many more assists. He moved to Tottenham at the age of 30 and won the PFA Player Of The Year in 1998, before spending time at Everton and Aston Villa.

35
ROBBIE FOWLER

PL Games: 379
PL Goals: 163
PL Assists: 39
PL Champion: 0
PL Clubs: Liverpool, Leeds, Man. City, Blackburn

Some players scored more, some had longer careers, but nobody in Premier League history scored so many goals as quickly as Robbie Fowler. The striker made his debut as a 17-year old and scored 13 goals in his first 12 games for the club, including a hat-trick in only his fifth game. By the time he turned 21, he had scored 64 Premier League goals, a record that still stands. Possibly one of the best finishers the Premier League has ever seen, it's telling that despite the great strikers Liverpool have had over the years, they still call Fowler 'God'.

37
TEDDY SHERINGHAM

PL Games: 418
PL Goals: 146
PL Assists: 76
PL Champion: 3
PL Clubs: Nottingham Forest, Tottenham, Man. United, Portsmouth, West Ham

Sheringham wasn't blessed with great pace, but he was an intelligent footballer who was often a step ahead of his opponents. He was able to drop deeper than a centre forward and provide assists as well as crucial goals. He won three Premier League titles at Man. United and became the oldest outfield player to score in a Premier League fixture at the age of 40.

34
N'GOLO KANTE

PL Games: 106
PL Goals: 3
PL Assists: 6
PL Champion 2
PL Clubs: Leicester, Chelsea

Despite only having played in the Premier League since 2015, the impact N'Golo Kante has had on the teams he's played for has been sensational. The France midfielder joined Leicester as a relative unknown but quickly became the fulcrum of the team on their way to winning the unlikeliest of Premier League titles. He joined Chelsea that summer, who had just finished 10th, and led them to the title the next season, winning the PFA Player Of The Year award in the process. His reading of the game, ability to break up play and work ethic is unsurpassed, and allows the players around him to flourish.

33
VINCENT KOMPANY

PL Games: 248
PL Goals: 17
PL Assists: 8
PL Champion: 3
PL Clubs: Man. City

When Kompany joined City in 2008 the club had a scattergun approach to signings, but it was instantly clear they'd bought well. Not only was the Belgian an excellent player, he was also a leader and a captain. At his peak, he was among the best centre-backs the Premier League has seen, and led the club to three titles. Injuries have taken their toll but tellingly, after nine years and hundreds of millions of pounds in expenditure, City are still no closer to finding a centre-back who is his equal.

32
JAAP STAM

PL Games: 79
PL Goals: 1
PL Assists: 2
PL Champion: 3
PL Clubs: Man. United

Stam was a defensive colossus for Man. United during a golden period for the club. He arrived at Old Trafford in a world record fee for a defender, but in his three seasons at the club he was part of the side that created history by winning the League, FA Cup and Champions League in 1999. Stam made only 79 appearances in the Premier League before being sold by Sir Alex Ferguson in 2001, though Fergie would later admit Stam's release was a mistake.

31
GARY NEVILLE

PL Games: 400
PL Goals: 5
PL Assists: 35
PL Champion: 8
PL Clubs: Man. United

Despite holding down the Man. United right-back spot for 15 years, winning eight Premier League titles and captaining the side for five years, Gary Neville is still one of the most under-rated players of the Premier League era. Aggressive, tenacious, with great positioning and reading of the game, Neville was the model of consistency, and was part of a United defence that kept 14 consecutive clean sheets between November 2008 and February 2009.

30
SOL CAMPBELL
PL Games: 503
PL Goals: 20
PL Assists: 15
PL Champion: 2
PL Clubs: Tottenham, Arsenal, Portsmouth, Newcastle

Campbell was a formidable opponent – a terrifying combination of strength, power, athleticism and intelligence. He was the rock at the heart of the Tottenham defence for six seasons before risking their wrath by joining north London rivals Arsenal. There, he won two Premier League titles in five seasons and was part of the 'Invincibles' team that went through the 2003-04 season unbeaten. He then moved to Portsmouth, who enjoyed their most successful spell in the Premier League with him in the team. It's no coincidence.

29
EDEN HAZARD
PL Games: 208
PL Goals: 61
PL Assists: 41
PL Champion: 2
PL Clubs: Chelsea

Since joining Chelsea from Lille as a 21-year-old in 2012, Hazard has developed into one of the most devastating talents in the Premier League. Surprisingly robust and physical for his size, he's also superb on the ball, able to ride challenges, dribble past opponents and burst past defenders. He's also got an eye for goals, and has reached double figures in four of his six full seasons at the club. He was Chelsea's best player in their title-winning seasons of 2015 and 2017 and, terrifyingly, his best years are still ahead of him.

28
MATT LE TISSIER
PL Games: 270
PL Goals: 100
PL Assists: 64
PL Champion: 0
PL Clubs: Southampton

It sounds incredible, but Southampton didn't win a single game in which Le Tissier didn't play for nearly five years during the 1990s, such was his influence in the side. He generally delivered when it mattered most – he converted 25 penalties in the Premier League – but it was the quality of his goals that he will be best remembered: 35-yard screamers, chipping the keeper or mazy dribbles – Le Tissier had the lot.

27
NEMANJA VIDIĆ
PL Games: 211
PL Goals: 15
PL Assists: 3
PL Champion: 5
PL Clubs: Man. United

Nemanja Vidić bore all the hallmarks of a traditional English defender: a towering leap, no frills and a total inability to feel pain. He and Rio Ferdinand became the best centre-back partnership of the Premier League era. United's 2008-09 side is remembered for the forward line of Tevez, Rooney, Ronaldo and Berbatov, but even more impressive was the defence which kept a 14 successive clean sheets that autumn.

26
ROBERT PIRES

PL Games: 198
PL Goals: 62
PL Assists: 41
PL Champion: 2
PL Clubs: Arsenal, Aston Villa

He may not have been the quickest winger, but Pires had a style and elegance to his game rarely seen in the Premier League. In 2001-02 he was devastatingly effective, the highlight being his lobbed goal over a bewildered Peter Schmeichel at Villa Park as Arsenal closed in on the Double. He was also part of Arsenal's 'Invincibles' of 2003-04 and although he had abrief spell with Aston Villa during the 2010-11 season, he will be forever remembered for his time at Arsenal.

25
LUIS SUAREZ

PL Games: 110
PL Goals: 69
PL Assists: 23
PL Champion: 0
PL Clubs: Liverpool

Suarez only played in the Premier League for three-and-a-half years, but the impact he had in that time demands his inclusion. Joining Liverpool on the same day as Andy Carroll, he enjoyed a rather better time at the club. The Uruguay striker's temperament was suspect, but his ability was without question. After scoring 11 goals in his first full season, he hit 23 in his next and then 31 in just 33 games as Liverpool went agonisingly close to winning their first Premier League title.

24
ASHLEY COLE

PL Games: 385
PL Goals: 15
PL Assists: 31
PL Champion: 3
PL Clubs: Arsenal, Chelsea

Ashley Cole was the first of a new generation of attacking full-backs who were just as happy to attack as to defend. Blessed with great pace, an ability to go past players and a good crosser of the ball, he was also sound defensively. He won two Premier League titles at Arsenal and was a key member of 'The Invincibles' side of 2003-04, before moving to Chelsea in 2006, where he won the Premier League again in 2009-10.

23
GARETH BALE

PL Games: 146
PL Goals: 42
PL Assists: 20
PL Champion: 0
PL Clubs: Tottenham

It's crazy to think that Bale had to wait two years before he won a Premier League game with Spurs. But after breaking that duck in September 2009, he went from strength to strength. Converted from a full-back into a flying winger with sensational effect, Bales's pace and ability to beat players, in addition to a left foot that was devastating from long range, and a mastery of set pieces, made him one of the most exciting players the Premier League has ever seen.

20
DAVID SILVA
PL Games: 249
PL Goals: 48
PL Assists: 75
PL Champion: 3
PL Clubs: Man. City

If you ask most Man. City fans they'll tell you Silva is the club's greatest ever player and it's difficult to argue. Since signing from Valencia in 2010, he has been the metronome in midfield for eight seasons, pulling strings, creating chances and scoring goals. City would have struggled to win their three Premier League titles without him in the side, such is his importance to the team.

22
DIDIER DROGBA
PL Games: 254
PL Goals: 104
PL Assists: 54
PL Champion: 4
PL Clubs: Chelsea

Drogba struggled initially after joining Chelsea from Marseille for £24 million in 2004, but once he became accustomed to his new surroundings he blossomed into one of the greatest strikers of the Premier League era. Strong, quick and with an eye for all types of goals, he was crucial in Chelsea's title wins under Jose Mourinho in 2004-05 and 2005-06 and again under Carlo Ancelotti in 2009-10, before returning to the club in 2014-15 to secure his fourth title.

21
SERGIO AGUERO
PL Games: 206
PL Goals: 143
PL Assists: 35
PL Champion: 3
PL Clubs: Man. City

Aguero is one of the greatest strikers of the Premier League era, and definitely the one to provide its greatest ever moment. His 94th minute strike to win Man. City their first Premier League title will be forever remembered, even though the Argentina star has now won two more with the club. In seven full seasons with the club he has amassed an incredible 143 goals, and hit 20 goals or more in five of those, and this despite missing a number of games through injury in the last few seasons.

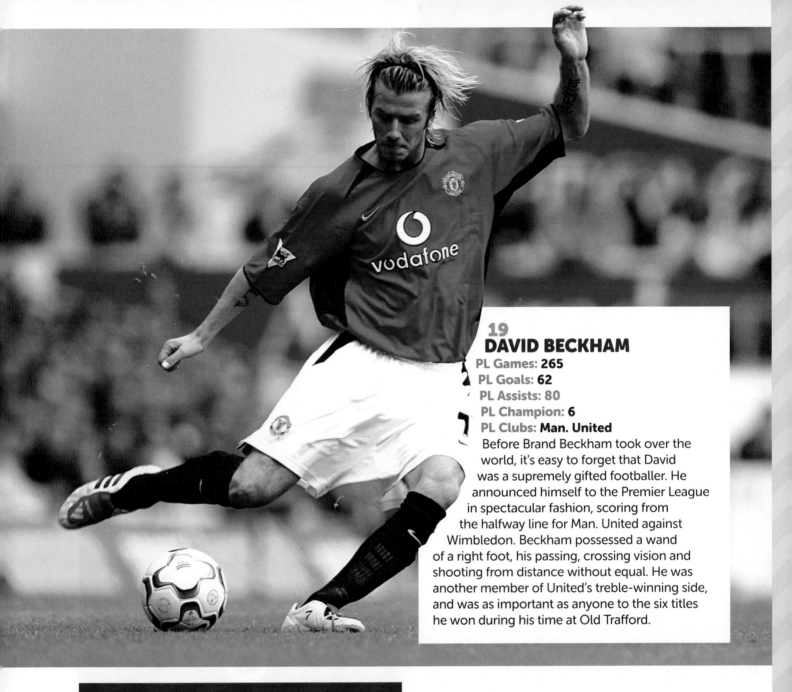

19
DAVID BECKHAM
PL Games: 265
PL Goals: 62
PL Assists: 80
PL Champion: 6
PL Clubs: Man. United

Before Brand Beckham took over the world, it's easy to forget that David was a supremely gifted footballer. He announced himself to the Premier League in spectacular fashion, scoring from the halfway line for Man. United against Wimbledon. Beckham possessed a wand of a right foot, his passing, crossing vision and shooting from distance without equal. He was another member of United's treble-winning side, and was as important as anyone to the six titles he won during his time at Old Trafford.

18
TONY ADAMS
PL Games: 255
PL Goals: 12
PL Assists: 9
PL Champion: 2
PL Clubs: Arsenal

Tony Adams was the ultimate one-club man and the rock at the heart of Arsenal's defence. The finest captain in Arsenal's history, he's also arguably the best the Premier League has ever seen. Adams was a supreme defender – the timing of his tackles, his reading of the game and his aerial ability were second to none, and he loved a battle. He captained a title-winning team in three decades, including the Premier League titles in 1998 and 2002, a feat which has never been repeated.

17
ANDREW COLE
PL Games: 414
PL Goals: 187
PL Assists: 73
PL Champion: 5
PL Clubs: Newcastle, Man. United, Blackburn, Fulham, Man. City, Portsmouth, Sunderland

Cole burst on to the Premier League scene in 1993-94, crashing in 34 goals in his first full season – still a Premier League record for 42 games. In 1995 he made a shock move to Man. United and after a slow start was an unqualified success, linking up with Eric Cantona, Dwight Yorke and Teddy Sheringham at different times as the Red Devils dominated the early years of the Premier League. In his time at United he won five titles, including the incredible Treble of 1998-99, before moving to Blackburn in 2001-02.

14
RIO FERDINAND
PL Games: 504
PL Goals: 11
PL Assists: 8
PL Champion: 6
PL Clubs: West Ham, Leeds, Man. United, QPR

Whereas John Terry was the archetypal English defender, Ferdinand had a more European style. Calm and confident on the ball, he could start attacks and had excellent distribution, but he also had great positional sense and timed his tackles to perfection. Ferdinand broke the British transfer record when he signed for Man. United in 2002 for £30 million, but six Premier League titles, three League cups and a Champions League winners' medal in 12 years at the club repaid that in spades and established him as one of the best defenders in world football.

16
PETER SCHMEICHEL
PL Games: 310
PL Clean Sheets: 128
PL Goals: 1
PL Champion: 5
PL Clubs: Man. United, Aston Villa, Man. City

Peter Schemichel is the greatest goalkeeper of the Premier League era. Brave, a born winner, commanding of his area and an incredible shot-stopper, Schmeichel won five titles in nine years at Old Trafford as United dominated the early years of the Premier League. He was as important as anyone in United's success in reasserting themselves as the best team in the country in the 1990s, and it is testament to him that the club struggled to find an adequate replacement for years after he left.

15
JOHN TERRY
PL Games: 492
PL Goals: 41
PL Assists: 12
PL Champion: 5
PL Clubs: Chelsea

One of a dying breed of old-fashioned centre-backs, John Terry was the rock around which Jose Mourinho built the title-winning teams of 2004-05 and 2005-06, their first for some 50 years. He stayed at the club until 2017 and led them to five Premier League titles, five FA Cups, three League Cups, the Champions League and the Europa League. A strong, physical defender, Terry was a born leader, the likes of which are becoming a rarity in the Premier League.

12
PATRICK VIEIRA
PL Games: 307
PL Goals: 31
PL Assists: 34
PL Champion: 3
PL Clubs: Arsenal, Man. City
Vieira joined Arsenal as an unknown 20-year old from Inter Milan in 1996, but left nine years later as a three-time Premier League winner, the captain of the great 'Invincibles' side of 2003-04 and one of the most respected midfielders in world football. His leadership, resilience, tenacity and ability under pressure were second to none, while his battles with great rival Roy Keane were utterly compelling.

11
GIANFRANCO ZOLA
PL Games: 229
PL Goals: 59
PL Assists: 42
PL Champion: 0
PL Clubs: Chelsea
Gianfranco Zola wasn't just an incredible player – he brought a professionalism and dedication that hadn't been seen before, and helped to educate team-mates as well as entertain the fans. On the pitch he was a magician who could do anything with a football – he could glide past players, had an incredible touch and took a brilliant free-kick. In 2003 he was named Chelsea's greatest ever player. What's more, he did all this with a smile and humility that endeared him to everyone.

13
FRANK LAMPARD
PL Games: 609
PL Goals: 177
PL Assists: 102
PL Champion: 3
PL Clubs: West Ham, Chelsea, Man. City
He may not have possessed the tenacity of Keane, the elegance of Scholes or the dynamism of Gerrard, but as a goalscoring midfielder Frank Lampard was without equal. He reached double figures ten seasons in a row in a Premier League total of 177, which sees him fourth in the list of all-time scorers. His ability to drive forward and score, or arrive in the penalty area at the right time to convert, was incredible, and he was a key member in the three titles he won at Chelsea, as well as the Champions League in 2012.

10
WAYNE ROONEY

PL Games: 491
PL Goals: 208
PL Assists: 103
PL Champion: 5
PL Clubs: Everton, Man. United

Few players have received such acclaim at such a young age, but then few players have possessed the ability of Wayne Rooney. A teen prodigy at Everton, Rooney became the world's most expensive teenager when he joined Man. United for £30 million at the age of 18. At Old Trafford he won five Premier League titles in a total 16 trophies, as well as the PFA Young Player Of The Year twice and the Player Of The Year award in 2010. Despite that, question marks remained as to whether he fulfilled his potential, but that is more a testament to just how brilliant he was as a young player.

9
ROY KEANE

PL Games: 366
PL Goals: 39
PL Assists: 33
PL Champion: 7
PL Clubs: Man. United

The £3.75 million Man. United spent on signing Roy Keane from Nottingham Forest in 1993 is arguably the best money they ever spent. Behind Sir Alex Ferguson himself, Keane was the next most important man in establishing United's Premier League dominance for the next ten years. In his time at the club they won two doubles and a treble, all the time driven on by their leader and captain Keane, whose relentless drive and will to win was the foundation on which United's success was built.

8
STEVEN GERRARD

PL Games: 504
PL Goals: 120
PL Assists: 92
PL Champion: 0
PL Clubs: Liverpool

Gerrard spent his entire Premier League career with the Reds and is surely the best player never to have lifted the trophy. He was the complete midfielder – box-to-box, able to play both holding and attacking roles, hard-working, had great vision, was a ball-winner, could tackle well, was strong in the air and possessed an incredible shot. Gerrard was made captain of the side at the age of just 23 and took the Reds agonisingly close to the title in 2009 and again in 2014, but ultimately the Premier League crown proved elusive.

7
PAUL SCHOLES

PL Games: 499
PL Goals: 107
PL Assists: 55
PL Champion: 11
PL Clubs: Man. United

Scholes made his debut for the Red Devils as a 19-year-old to become one of the greatest players United, and the Premier League, has seen. At times under-rated, Scholes was blessed with superb technical ability, great vision, a superb range of passing and an ability to score from distance. He won ten Premier League titles before retiring in May 2011, only to return in January 2012 and win an 11th title in the 2012-13 season.

6
DENNIS BERGKAMP

PL Games: 315
PL Goals: 87
PL Assists: 94
PL Champion: 3
PL Clubs: Arsenal

A Bruce Rioch signing, Bergkamp attracted attention as being one of the first overseas players to arrive in the Premier League with his best years ahead of him. Under Arsène Wenger he proved that, becoming the perfect foil to firstly Ian Wright, and later Thierry Henry. His technical ability, control, awareness and ability to bring others into the game was something the Premier League hadn't seen before, and has rarely since. The Gunners won three titles and three FA Cups with him in the team, a feat unimaginable without him.

5
ALAN SHEARER

PL Games: 441
PL Goals: 260
PL Assists: 64
PL Champion: 1
PL Clubs: Blackburn, Newcastle

Shearer is the Premier League's greatest ever goalscorer by far, and if it hadn't been for a succession of serious injuries during his career, his incredible total of 260 Premier League goals in 441 games could have been so much higher. He joined Blackburn in the inaugural Premier League season for a British record £3.6 million in 1992 and quickly made that look a bargain, becoming the only player to score 30 goals or more in three consecutive Premier League seasons and shooting Blackburn to an unlikely title win in 1994-95. He moved to boyhood club Newcastle in 1996 and despite not being able to help the Magpies to a trophy, became a club legend for his unrelenting goalscoring and passion for the club.

4
ERIC CANTONA

PL Games: 156
PL Goals: 70
PL Assists: 56
PL Champion: 4
PL Clubs: Leeds, Man. United

Cantona joined Man. United from rivals Leeds, who he had just helped return to the top-flight title the previous May. The France star quickly established himself as one of, if not the, key player in United's dominance at the start of the Premier League era. He brought style, imagination and the unexpected to the side. His control, vision, grace and ability to do what others could only dream of complemented United's other strengths perfectly, and in four-and-a-half years at Old Trafford he won the Premier League title four times. A true great.

3
RYAN GIGGS

PL Games: 632
PL Goals: 109
PL Assists: 162
PL Champion: 13
PL Clubs: Man. United

Ryan Giggs is a Premier League legend in every sense of the word. He played in every one of the first 22 seasons, scoring in the first 21, but there is far more to his legacy than longevity alone. His astonishing total of 13 titles will surely never be matched, and the way he developed and changed his game over the years was better than anyone else has managed. From a flying winger with electric pace in the 1990s and early 2000s to a more refined, intelligent midfield role, it says everything that his only PFA Player Of The Year award came in 2008-09, when Giggs was 35.

CRISTIANO RONALDO

PL Games: 196
PL Goals: 84
PL Assists: 34
PL Champion: 3
PL Clubs: Man. United

Cristiano Ronaldo arrived at Man. United as an 18-year-old and left six years later with nine trophies, including three Premier League titles, as arguably the best player in the world. He scored 84 goals in 196 games, mainly from the right wing, but like Giggs, developed his game at United to become a more rounded attacking player, ending his time there almost as a second centre-forward. A supreme athlete, Ronaldo was blessed with power, pace, unbelievable tricks, superb aerial ability and a drive to improve that was an obsession. The only regret is that the League didn't get to see him in his prime in the way Real Madrid did, but those six years were more than enough to cement his place in the list of all-time Premier League greats.

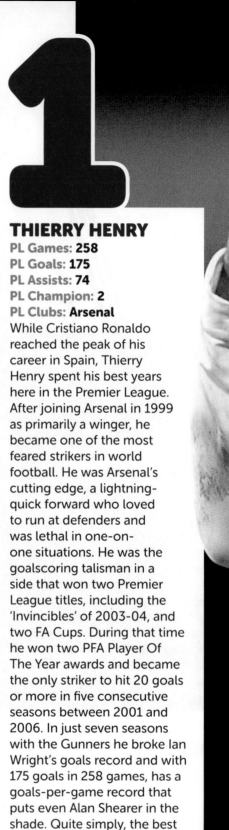

THIERRY HENRY

PL Games: 258
PL Goals: 175
PL Assists: 74
PL Champion: 2
PL Clubs: Arsenal

While Cristiano Ronaldo reached the peak of his career in Spain, Thierry Henry spent his best years here in the Premier League. After joining Arsenal in 1999 as primarily a winger, he became one of the most feared strikers in world football. He was Arsenal's cutting edge, a lightning-quick forward who loved to run at defenders and was lethal in one-on-one situations. He was the goalscoring talisman in a side that won two Premier League titles, including the 'Invincibles' of 2003-04, and two FA Cups. During that time he won two PFA Player Of The Year awards and became the only striker to hit 20 goals or more in five consecutive seasons between 2001 and 2006. In just seven seasons with the Gunners he broke Ian Wright's goals record and with 175 goals in 258 games, has a goals-per-game record that puts even Alan Shearer in the shade. Quite simply, the best the Premier League has ever seen.

WHAT THEY SAY...

Here's what fellow players and managers have to say about Henry...

"The first day that he came into the dressing room, I did not dare to look him in the face. I knew everything that he had done in England."
BARCELONA TEAM-MATE LIONEL MESSI

"It was like he was playing a different game at times. He used to glide, he was so smooth. The way he used to run down the left, cut inside and bend one into the corner was amazing. If you closed your eyes you could picture him doing it time after time. He was an incredible footballer, scored unbelievable goals and if you had him in your team you would have won league after league. He had a sensational appetite to win. There have been some brilliant Premier League players — Frank Lampard, Steven Gerrard, Alan Shearer, Roy Keane, Patrick Vieira — but Henry was the one."
FORMER TOTTENHAM & LIVERPOOL STAR JAMIE REDKNAPP

"I am a huge fan of Roy Keane — he was very influential in that unbelievable Manchester United era — and Alan Shearer's goals put him up there, but the best has to be Henry. Not only was he the best player in the Premier League, he was the best player in world football for a period. You could not say that about many others. In the Invincible team he was unplayable. The goals he scored and the threat he was in that Arsenal team were absolutely sensational."
FORMER BLACKBURN & CHELSEA STRIKER CHRIS SUTTON

"It was embarrassing for the defenders. He just scored when he wanted."
FORMER MANAGER ARSENE WENGER

"Thierry Henry would play for Arsenal like he was a 20-year-old playing in an Under-12 league, and I've never seen that before."
FORMER ARSENAL STAR PAUL MERSON

"Thierry Henry is probably technically the most gifted footballer ever to play the beautiful game."
FORMER FRANCE TEAM-MATE ZINEDINE ZIDANE

"I've used this analogy before and I make no apology for using it again. When he hit top gear and ran past you, it was like trying to chase after someone on a motorbike. When Arsenal were 'The Invincibles' in the period between 2003-2004, Henry rivalled Ronaldinho as the best in the world. A great goal-scorer, not to mention a scorer of great goals, he is the finest player I have seen in the Premier League. His game didn't have a weakness."
FORMER LIVERPOOL DEFENDER JAMIE CARRAGHER

PREMIER LEAGUE
TOP TENS

Let's face it – everybody loves a list, and everybody loves a statistic. And if you're reading this, the chances are you love the Premier League too. So here's a load of lists of statistics on the Premier League, from goalscorers to transfers, appearances to assists, and everything in between.

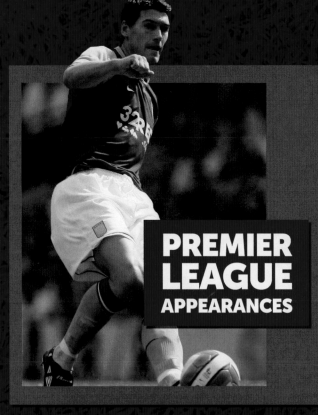

PREMIER LEAGUE APPEARANCES

1.	Gareth **Barry**	653
2.	Ryan **Giggs**	632
3.	Frank **Lampard**	609
4.	David **James**	572
5.	Gary **Speed**	535
6.	Emile **Heskey**	516
7.	Mark **Schwarzer**	514
8.	Jamie **Carragher**	508
9.	Phil **Neville**	505
10.	Rio **Ferdinand**	504

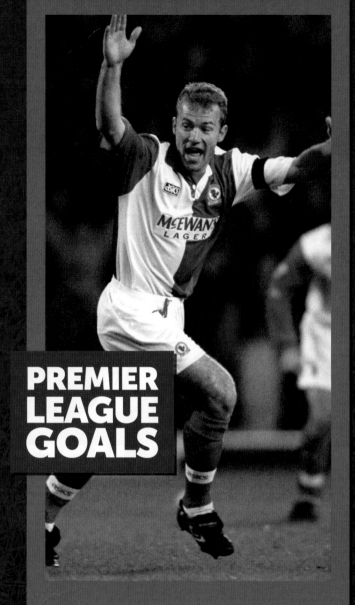

PREMIER LEAGUE GOALS

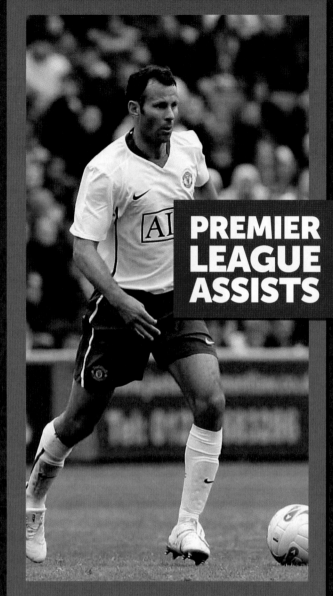

PREMIER LEAGUE ASSISTS

1.	Alan **Shearer**	260
2.	Wayne **Rooney**	208
3.	Andrew **Cole**	187
4.	Frank **Lampard**	177
5.	Thierry **Henry**	175
6.	Robbie **Fowler**	163
7.	Jermain **Defoe**	162
8.	Michael **Owen**	150
9.	Les **Ferdinand**	149
10.	Teddy **Sheringham**	149

1.	Ryan **Giggs**	162
2.	Cesc **Fabregas**	111
3.	Andrew **Cole**	103
4.	Wayne **Rooney**	102
5.	Dennis **Bergkamp**	94
6.	Steven **Gerrard**	92
7.	David **Beckham**	80
8.	James **Milner**	79
9.	Teddy **Sheringham**	76
10.	David **Silva**	75

* Stats correct up to August 24, 2018.

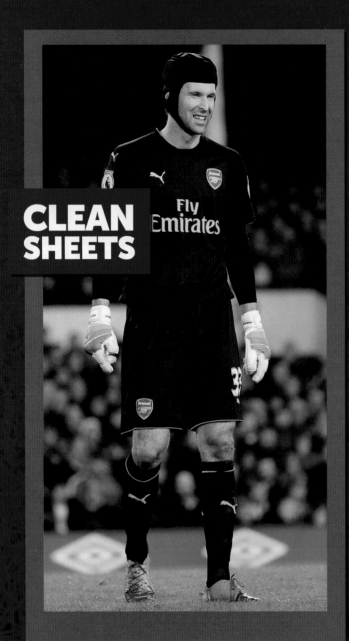

CLEAN SHEETS

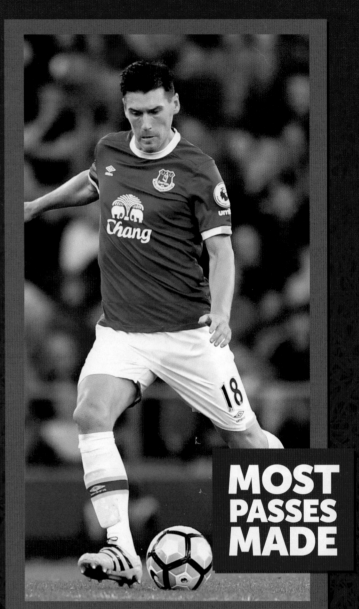

MOST PASSES MADE

	CLEAN SHEETS	
1.	Petr **Čech**	201
2.	David **James**	169
3.	Mark **Schwarzer**	151
4.	David **Seaman**	140
5.	Nigel **Martyn**	137
6.	Pepe **Reina**	134
7=	Edwin **van der Sar**	132
7=	Tim **Howard**	132
7=	Brad **Friedel**	132
10.	Peter **Schmeichel**	128

	MOST PASSES MADE	
1.	Gareth **Barry**	20,616
2.	Cesc **Fabregas**	18,994
3.	Michael **Carrick**	18,978
4.	Yaya **Touré**	15,744
5.	David **Silva**	15,356
6.	Steven **Gerrard**	15,108
7.	Gael **Clichy**	15,076
8.	Mark **Noble**	14,936
9.	John **Terry**	14,765
10.	Wayne **Rooney**	14,693

MOST YELLOW CARDS

1.	Gareth **Barry**	125
2.	Wayne **Rooney**	101
3.	Lee **Bowyer**	100
4=	Kevin **Davies**	99
4=	Paul **Scholes**	99
6.	Scott **Parker**	92
7.	Lee **Cattermole**	91
8.	Robbie **Savage**	87
9.	George **Boateng**	87
10.	Kevin **Nolan**	86

MOST FOULS

1.	Gareth **Barry**	633
2.	Kevin **Davies**	605
3.	Marouane **Fellaini**	573
4.	Gabriel **Agbonlahor**	439
5=	Lee **Cattermole**	422
5=	Peter **Crouch**	422
7.	Antonio **Valencia**	419
8.	Lucas **Leiva**	410
9.	James **Milner**	403
10.	Tim **Cahill**	402

MOST TOUCHES

1.	Gareth **Barry**	27,238
2.	Leighton **Baines**	25,367
3.	Cesc **Fabregas**	24,168
4.	Gael **Clichy**	23,444
5.	Michael **Carrick**	22,525
6.	James **Milner**	22,038
7.	Bacary **Sagna**	21,068
8.	Glen **Johnson**	21,039
9.	Steven **Gerrard**	20,750
10.	Wayne **Rooney**	20,714

MOST SHOTS

1.	Wayne **Rooney**	1,237
2.	Jermain **Defoe**	870
3.	Robin **van Persie**	862
4.	Frank **Lampard**	832
5.	Sergio **Aguero**	814
6.	Steven **Gerrard**	743
7.	Didier **Drogba**	663
8.	Peter **Crouch**	638
9.	Stewart **Downing**	630
10.	Romelu **Lukaku**	629

* Stats correct up to August 24, 2018.

HIGHEST POINTS TOTAL

1.	Man. City (2017-18)	100
2.	Chelsea (2004-05)	95
3.	Chelsea (2016-17)	93
4.	Man. United (1993-94)	92
5=	Man. United (1999-00)	91
5=	Chelsea (2005-06)	91
7=	Arsenal (2003-04)	90
7=	Man. United (2008-09)	90
9=	Blackburn (1994-95)	89
9=	Man. United (2006-07)	89
9=	Man. City (2011-12)	89
9=	Man. United (2011-12)	89

BIGGEST STADIUMS

* Clubs do not need to be currently in the Premier League

1.	Old Trafford	Man. United	75,731
2.	London Stadium	West Ham	66,000
3.	Tottenham Hotspur Stadium	Tottenham	62,062
4.	Emirates Stadium	Arsenal	60,432
5.	Etihad Stadium	Man. City	55,097
6.	Anfield	Liverpool	54,074
7.	St James' Park	Newcastle	52,404
8.	Stadium Of Light	Sunderland	49,000
9.	Villa Park	Aston Villa	42,573
10.	Stamford Bridge	Chelsea	41,841

PREMIER LEAGUE TRANSFERS

1.	Paul **Pogba**	Juventus to Man. United	£93.25m
2=	Romelu **Lukaku**	Everton to Man. United	£75m
2=	Virgil **van Dijk**	Southampton to Liverpool	£75m
4.	Kepa **Arrizabalaga**	Athletic Bilbao to Chelsea	£71.6m
5.	Alvaro **Morata**	Real Madrid to Chelsea	£70m
6.	Alisson **Becker**	Roma to Liverpool	£67m
7.	**Fred**	Shakhtar to Man. United	£61.2m
8=	PE **Aubameyang**	B. Dortmund to Arsenal	£60m
8=	Riyad **Mahrez**	Leicester to Man. City	£60m
10.	Angel **Di Maria**	Real Madrid to Man. United	£59.7m

MOST GOALS IN A PL SEASON (38 GAMES)

1.	Mohamed **Salah**	Liverpool (2017-18)	32
2=	Alan **Shearer**	Blackburn (1994-95)	31
2=	Cristiano **Ronaldo**	Man. United (2007-08)	31
2=	Luis **Suarez**	Liverpool (2013-14)	31
5=	Kevin **Phillips**	Sunderland (1999-00)	30
5=	Thierry **Henry**	Arsenal (2003-04)	30
5=	Robin **van Persie**	Arsenal (2011-12)	30
8=	Didier **Drogba**	Chelsea (2009-10)	29
8=	Harry **Kane**	Tottenham (2016-17)	29
10=	Thierry **Henry**	Arsenal (2005-06)	27
10=	Wayne **Rooney**	Man. United (2011-12)	27

MOST HEADED GOALS

1.	Peter **Crouch**	40
2.	Olivier **Giroud**	29
3.	Christian **Benteke**	25
4.	Andy **Carroll**	24
5=	Tim **Cahill**	22
5=	Kenwyne **Jones**	22
5=	Romelu **Lukaku**	22
8.	Wayne **Rooney**	21
9.	Emmanuel **Adebayor**	20
10.	Steven **Fletcher**	19

MOST PENALTIES SCORED

1.	Frank **Lampard**	32
2.	Steven **Gerrard**	29
3.	Wayne **Rooney**	23
4.	Sergio **Aguero**	22
5=	Leighton **Baines**	20
5=	Mark **Noble**	20
7.	Mikel **Arteta**	17
8.	Robin **van Persie**	15
9=	Gareth **Barry**	14
9=	Darren **Bent**	14
9=	Jermain **Defoe**	14
9=	Harry **Kane**	14

MOST PREMIER LEAGUE HAT-TRICKS

1.	Alan **Shearer**	11
2=	Sergio **Aguero**	9
2=	Robbie **Fowler**	9
4.	Michael **Owen**	8
5.	Harry **Kane**	8
6.	Wayne **Rooney**	7
7.	Luis **Suarez**	6
8=	Dimitar **Berbatov**	5
8=	Ruud **van Nistelrooy**	5
8=	Andrew **Cole**	5

MOST GOALS CONCEDED

1.	Ben **Foster**	399
2.	Tim **Howard**	385
3.	Jussi **Jääskeläinen**	377
4.	Robert **Green**	357
5.	Joe **Hart**	345
6.	Paul **Robinson**	340
7.	Petr **Cech**	329
8.	Mark **Schwarzer**	318
9.	Simon **Mignolet**	311
10.	Brad **Friedel**	306

HIT WOODWORK

1.	Robin **van Persie**	44
2.	Wayne **Rooney**	29
3=	Steven **Gerrard**	26
3=	Luis **Suarez**	26
5.	Jermain **Defoe**	23
6=	Sergio **Aguero**	22
6=	Peter **Crouch**	22
8.	Fernando **Torres**	21
9=	Stewart **Downing**	20
9=	Harry **Kane**	20

OWN GOALS

1.	Richard **Dunne**	10
2=	Jamie **Carragher**	7
2=	Martin **Skrtel**	7
4=	Wes **Brown**	6
4=	Phil **Jagielka**	6
4=	Ryan **Shawcross**	6
4=	Frank **Sinclair**	6
8=	Ten Players	5

* Stats correct up to August 24, 2018.

1.	Man. United	1924
2.	Arsenal	1772
3.	Chelsea	1707
4.	Liverpool	1685
5.	Tottenham	1480
6.	Everton	1303
7.	Man. City	1279
8.	Newcastle	1207
9.	Aston Villa	1117
10.	West Ham	1012

TOP-SCORING PREMIER LEAGUE TEAMS

1.	Man. City (2017-18)	351
2.	Chelsea (2009-10)	348
3.	Man. City (2013-14)	333
4.	Liverpool (2013-14)	323
5.	Man. United (1999-00)	322
6.	Man. City (2011-12)	303
7.	Man. United (2011-12)	296
8=	Man. United (2001-02)	257
8=	Arsenal (2003-04)	250
10=	Man. United (2009-10)	246
10=	Man. United (2009-10)	246

MOST TEAM GOALS IN A SEASON

MOST PREMIER LEAGUE WINS

1.	Man. United	629
2.	Arsenal	544
3.	Chelsea	537
4.	Liverpool	499
5.	Tottenham	423
6.	Everton	362
7.	Man. City	359
8.	Newcastle	334
9.	Aston Villa	316
10.	West Ham	275

MOST PREMIER LEAGUE DEFEATS

1.	Everton	351
2.	West Ham	348
3.	Aston Villa	333
4.	Newcastle	323
5.	Tottenham	322
6.	Southampton	303
7.	Sunderland	296
8.	Man. City	257
9.	Blackburn	250
10.	Liverpool	246

THE PREMIER LEAGUE'S ALL TIME TABLE

Since the Premier League began in 1992-93, a total of 49 clubs have played in the competition. Six teams – Man. United, Arsenal, Chelsea, Liverpool, Tottenham and Everton – have played in every season since its inception, while all the rest have been relegated at some point.

But which club is the best in Premier League history? If you added up every single point they won over all the seasons they've spent in the Premier League, who would finish top? Which clubs would make a 20-team league? The numbers are mind-boggling, but here's the countdown from 20 to one.

20 STOKE CITY

The Potters were promoted to the Premier League in 2008 and enjoyed ten uninterrupted years in the top flight, mainly under Tony Pulis, before suffering relegation last season. During that time they won 31% of their games, averaging over 45 points per season. They finished 9th in 2013-14, their highest Premier League finish.

Seasons:	10	Winners:	0
Played:	380	2nd:	0
Won:	116	3rd:	0
Drawn:	109	4th:	0
Lost:	155	Relegated:	1
Goals For:	398	Av. Points:	45.70
Goals Against:	525	Highest Finish:	9th
Points:	457		

19 WEST BROMWICH ALBION

West Brom are one of the Premier League's yo-yo teams, winning promotion to the top flight three times and being relegated four, which is a joint record. They first came up in 2002, but more recently enjoyed eight seasons in the top flight from 2010 to 2018, and came an impressive 8th, their best finish, in 2012.

Seasons:	12	Winners:	0
Played:	456	2nd:	0
Won:	112	3rd:	0
Drawn:	128	4th:	0
Lost:	216	Relegated:	4
Goals For:	475	Av. Points:	38.67
Goals Against:	696	Highest Finish:	8th
Points:	464		

18 LEICESTER CITY

Even though they average just over 46 points and have only been in the Premier League for 12 seasons, the Foxes are one of only six teams to have won the title. Leicester enjoyed four consecutive top-ten finishes under Martin O'Neill in the late 1990s but then spent ten years outside the top flight, returning in 2014.

Seasons:	12	Winners:	1
Played:	460	2nd:	0
Won:	142	3rd:	0
Drawn:	129	4th:	0
Lost:	189	Relegated:	3
Goals For:	572	Av. Points:	46.25
Goals Against:	670	Highest Finish:	1st
Points:	555		

17 BOLTON WANDERERS

Bolton rose from the third tier of English football in 1992-93 to take their place in the 1995-96 Premier League. The Trotters moved between the two divisions for the next few years before spending 11 consecutive seasons in the top division between 2001 and 2012, including a 6th place finish in 2005 under Sam Allardyce.

Seasons:	13	Goals For:	575	3rd:	0
Played:	494	Goals Ag.:	745	4th:	0
Won:	149	Points:	575	Relegated:	3
Drawn:	128	Winners:	0	Av. Points:	44.23
Lost:	217	2nd:	0	Highest Finish:	6th

16 FULHAM

Fulham were in the fourth tier of English football in 1996-97, but rose to take their place in the 2001-02 Premier League. The Cottagers then enjoyed 13 uninterrupted seasons in the top flight, including a 7th place finish in 2008-09 under Roy Hodgson while averaging just over 45 points per season. They were relegated in 2013-14 but won promotion back to the Premier League in 2018.

Seasons:	13	Goals For:	570	3rd:	0
Played:	494	Goals Ag.:	697	4th:	0
Won:	150	Points:	586	Relegated:	4
Drawn:	136	Winners:	0	Av. Points:	45.09
Lost:	208	2nd:	0	Highest Finish:	7th

15 SUNDERLAND

Despite spending 16 seasons in the Premier League, the Black Cats have also suffered relegation four times, which is a joint record. They first won promotion to the Premier League in 1995-96 and enjoyed their best spell during the 1999-2000 and 2000-01 seasons, where they finished 7th two years in a row.

Seasons:	16	Goals For:	612	3rd:	0
Played:	608	Goals Ag.:	904	4th:	0
Won:	153	Points:	618	Relegated:	4
Drawn:	159	Winners:	0	Av. Points:	38.63
Lost:	296	2nd:	0	Highest Finish:	7th

14 MIDDLESBROUGH

Middlesbrough took part in the first ever Premier League season after winning promotion from Division 2 in 1991-92. The club have been relegated a joint-record four times, but enjoyed 11 years in the league between 1998-99 and 2008-09 and enjoyed their highest finish in 2004-05, when they finished 7th under Steve McClaren.

Seasons:	15	Goals For:	648	3rd:	0
Played:	574	Goals Ag.:	794	4th:	0
Won:	165	Points:	661	Relegated:	4
Drawn:	169	Winners:	0	Av. Points:	44.01
Lost:	240	2nd:	0	Highest Finish:	7th

13 LEEDS UNITED

Leeds were First Division champions the season before the Premier League began, but haven't been able to repeat such a feat since. The Whites finished fifth or above in seven of the nine seasons between 1993-94 and 2001-02, including third place in 1999-2000, but after suffering relegation in 2004 they haven't made it back to the top flight.

Seasons:	12	Winners:	1	
Played:	468	2nd:	0	
Won:	189	3rd:	1	
Drawn:	125	4th:	2	
Lost:	154	Relegated:	1	
Goals For:	641	Av. Points:	57.67	
Goals Against:	573	Highest Finish:	3rd	
Points:	692			

12 SOUTHAMPTON

Southampton only won promotion back to the Premier League in 2012 following a seven-year absence, but before that had been founder members and ever present. Though they were often in the lower reaches during their first spell in the League, they have enjoyed four top-half finishes since 2013-14, including sixth place in 2016.

Seasons:	19	Winners:	0
Played:	734	2nd:	0
Won:	229	3rd:	0
Drawn:	202	4th:	0
Lost:	303	Relegated:	1
Goals For:	892	Av. Points:	46.79
Goals Against:	1022	Highest Finish:	6th
Points:	889		

11 BLACKBURN ROVERS

It's hard to believe now, but Blackburn were one of the powerhouses of English football at the start of the Premier League era. They won promotion in 1991-92 to play in the first Premier League season, finishing fourth. Rovers were runners-up the following year, before winning the title in their third. They could never reach those heights again, but still average a healthy 53.89 points each season.

Seasons:	18	Winners:	1
Played:	696	2nd:	0
Won:	262	3rd:	0
Drawn:	184	4th:	1
Lost:	250	Relegated:	2
Goals For:	927	Av. Points:	53.89
Goals Against:	907	Highest Finish:	1st
Points:	970		

10 WEST HAM UNITED

The Hammers are the only club from the all-time Premier League table's Top Ten to have never reached the top four. But their strength has been consistency, having spent 22 out of the 26 seasons in the top division and enjoying four top-half finishes out of five between 1998 and 2002, including fifth place in the 1998-99 season under Harry Redknapp.

Seasons:	22	Winners:	0
Played:	844	2nd:	0
Won:	275	3rd:	0
Drawn:	221	4th:	0
Lost:	348	Relegated:	2
Goals For:	1012	Av. Points:	47.55
Goals Against:	1214	Highest Finish:	5th
Points:	1046		

9 ASTON VILLA

Aston Villa were one of only seven clubs to have played in the first 24 seasons of the Premier League before suffering relegation in 2016. The Villans were runners-up to Man. United in their first ever Premier League season, claimed fourth spot in 1995-96, and achieved 15 top-half finishes in the first 19 years, with eight of those in the top six.

Seasons:	24
Played:	924
Won:	316
Drawn:	275
Lost:	333
Goals For:	1186
Goals Against:	1186
Points:	1223
Winners:	0
2nd:	1
3rd:	0
4th:	1
Relegated:	1
Av. Points:	50.96
Highest Finish:	2nd

8 NEWCASTLE UTD

Newcastle won promotion to the Premier League in 1992-93 and finished third the following season, establishing themselves as one of the most exciting teams around under manager Kevin Keegan. They squandered a 12-point lead at the top of the table to finish second to Man. United in 1995-96, and finished runners-up again in 1996-97.

Seasons:	23	Winners:	0
Played:	882	2nd:	2
Won:	334	3rd:	2
Drawn:	225	4th:	1
Lost:	323	Relegated:	2
Goals For:	1207	Av. Points:	53.35
Goals Against:	1187	Highest Finish:	2nd
Points:	1227		

7 MAN. CITY

It's amazing to think that in the early years of the Premier League, City were one of the perennial strugglers. They were relegated in 1998 and again in 2001, and have only been top-four contenders since 2009-10. But after winning their first PL title in 2011-12, they've won it twice since and in 2017-18 became the first team to reach 100 points.

Seasons:	21	Goals For:	1279	3rd:	2
Played:	810	Goals Ag.:	952	4th:	1
Won:	359	Points:	1271	Relegated:	2
Drawn:	194	Winners:	3	Av. Points:	60.52
Lost:	257	2nd:	2	Highest Finish:	1st

6 EVERTON

Everton are one of only six teams to have played in every season of the Premier League since it began in 1992, and hold the unenviable record for the most draws and defeats. In 2004-05 the club finished fourth, their highest in the Premier League era, which meant they qualified for the following season's Champions League, despite finishing with a negative goal difference.

Seasons:	26	Goals For:	1301	3rd:	0
Played:	1000	Goals Ag.:	1265	4th:	1
Won:	362	Points:	1373	Relegated:	0
Drawn:	287	Winners:	0	Av. Points:	52.81
Lost:	351	2nd:	0	Highest Finish:	4th

5 TOTTENHAM HOTSPUR

Tottenham were one of the founder members of the Premier League and have played in every single year since its inception. The club have conceded a record 1267 Premier League goals, but since the 2003-04 season the club have only finished outside the top ten once. Since 2014-15, they have finished third, second and third again, winning 42% of their games with an average of 1.53 points per game.

Seasons:	26	Winners:	0
Played:	1000	2nd:	1
Won:	432	3rd:	2
Drawn:	255	4th:	2
Lost:	322	Relegated:	0
Goals For:	1480	Av. Points:	58.62
Goals Against:	1267	Highest Finish:	2nd
Points:	1524		

4 LIVERPOOL

Remarkably, Liverpool are fourth in the all-time Premier League table, despite the fact they have never lifted the title. The last time the Reds won the top flight was in 1990, two years before the Premier League was formed. Since then they've finished runners-up three times, and third and fourth a joint-record five and seven times respectively.

Seasons:	26	Goals For:	1685	3rd:	5
Played:	1000	Goals Ag.:	1024	4th:	7
Won:	499	Points:	1752	Relegated:	0
Drawn:	255	Winners:	0	Av. Points:	67.38
Lost:	246	2nd:	3	Highest Finish:	2nd

3 CHELSEA

Considering the success Chelsea have enjoyed in recent years, it's hard to believe they were a mid-table team during the first few years of the Premier League, finishing 11th three times and 14th, in its first four years. But that all changed with Roman Abramovich, and after the club won their first title in 2004-05, they went on to claim it on four more occasions to elevate them to third in the all-time table.

Seasons:	26	Winners:	5
Played:	1000	2nd:	4
Won:	537	3rd:	4
Drawn:	248	4th:	2
Lost:	215	Relegated:	0
Goals For:	1707	Av. Points:	71.50
Goals Against:	693	Highest Finish:	1st
Points:	1859		

2 ARSENAL

Arsenal's last title win was in 2003-04, some 14 years ago, but they're still second in the all-time table. That's down to their consistency of finishing in the top four each year, especially under Arsene Wenger, who helped the Gunners to 20 consecutive top-four finishes between 1997 and 2016. They share the record of six runners-up spots with Man. United, five third place and seven fourth place finishes with Liverpool.

Seasons:	26	Winners:	3
Played:	1000	2nd:	6
Won:	544	3rd:	5
Drawn:	253	4th:	7
Lost:	203	Relegated:	0
Goals For:	1772	Av. Points:	72.50
Goals Against:	962	Highest Finish:	1st
Points:	1885		

1 MAN. UNITED

United haven't won the title since 2012-13, but at the end of the 2017-18 season they'd still amassed 117 more points than their nearest rival, Arsenal. That's down to the Old Trafford club's dominance in the early days of the competition, when they won seven out of the first nine years of the Premier League and have only finished out of the top four in three seasons. United also hold the record for the most wins, most title wins, most goals scored and the best goal difference.

Seasons:	26	Goals For:	1924	3rd:	3
Played:	1000	Goals Against:	875	4th:	1
Won:	629	Points:	2012	Relegated:	0
Drawn:	215	Winners:	13	Av. Points:	80.85
Lost:	156	2nd:	6	Highest Finish:	1st

		P	W	D	L	F	A	GD	PTS
1	Man. United	1000	629	215	156	1924	875	1049	2102
2	Arsenal	1000	544	253	203	1772	962	810	1885
3	Chelsea	1000	537	248	215	1707	963	744	1859
4	Liverpool	1000	499	255	246	1685	1024	661	1752
5	Tottenham	1000	423	255	322	1480	1267	213	1524
6	Everton	1000	362	287	351	1303	1265	38	1373
7	Man. City	810	359	194	257	1279	952	327	1271
8	Newcastle	882	334	225	323	1207	1187	20	1227
9	Aston Villa	924	316	275	333	1117	1186	-69	1223
10	West Ham	844	275	221	348	1012	1214	-202	1046
11	Blackburn	696	262	184	250	927	907	20	970
12	Southampton	734	229	202	303	892	1022	-130	889
13	Leeds	468	189	125	154	641	573	68	692
14	Middlesbrough	574	165	169	240	648	794	-146	661
15	Sunderland	608	153	159	296	612	904	-292	618
16	Fulham	494	150	136	208	570	697	-127	586
17	Bolton	494	149	128	217	575	745	-170	575
18	Leicester	460	142	129	189	573	670	-98	555
19	West Brom	456	112	128	216	475	696	-221	464
20	Stoke	380	116	109	155	398	525	-127	457

THE TEN
GREATEST PREMIER LEAGUE GAMES
OF ALL TIME!

At the end of the 2017/18 season, a total of 10,126 Premier League games had been played. As any fan will concede, some games are better than others. Some are instantly forgettable, some are memorable for all the wrong reasons, but occasionally, just occasionally, there's a game that is totally captivating. A game so absorbing, so full of incident, magical moments, or controversy that it reminds you why this is the beautiful game, the best game on the planet. Here are the Ten Best Premier League Games of All-Time. Many will disagree, but then, that's why football's so great, isn't it?

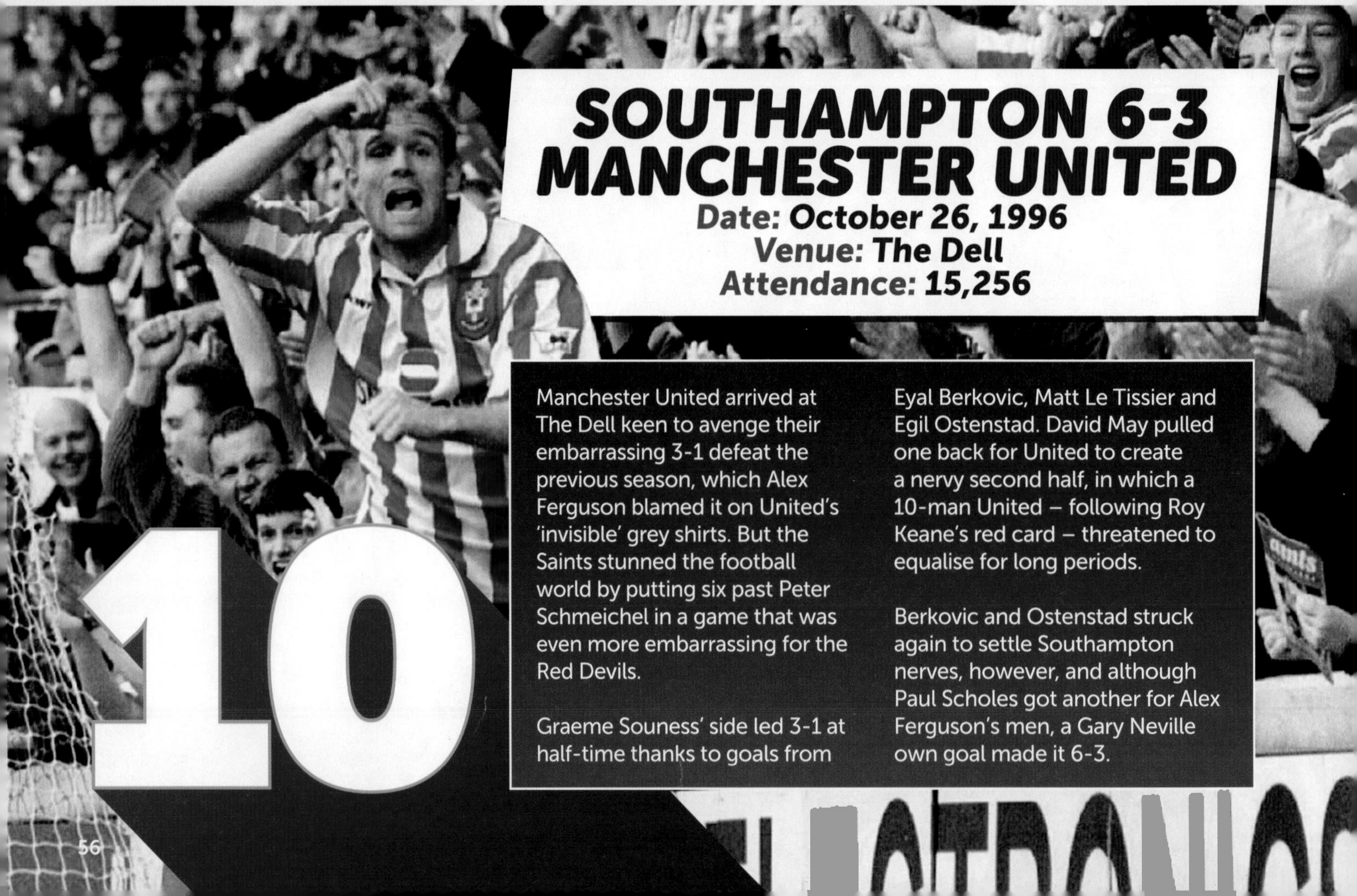

SOUTHAMPTON 6-3 MANCHESTER UNITED

Date: October 26, 1996
Venue: The Dell
Attendance: 15,256

10

Manchester United arrived at The Dell keen to avenge their embarrassing 3-1 defeat the previous season, which Alex Ferguson blamed it on United's 'invisible' grey shirts. But the Saints stunned the football world by putting six past Peter Schmeichel in a game that was even more embarrassing for the Red Devils.

Graeme Souness' side led 3-1 at half-time thanks to goals from Eyal Berkovic, Matt Le Tissier and Egil Ostenstad. David May pulled one back for United to create a nervy second half, in which a 10-man United – following Roy Keane's red card – threatened to equalise for long periods.

Berkovic and Ostenstad struck again to settle Southampton nerves, however, and although Paul Scholes got another for Alex Ferguson's men, a Gary Neville own goal made it 6-3.

MANCHESTER UNITED 1-6 MANCHESTER CITY
Date: October 23, 2011 Venue: Old Trafford
Attendance: 75,487

9

In October 2011, Manchester City travelled across the city to Old Trafford looking to demonstrate their title credentials — and they left having done so in emphatic fashion.

After a cagey start, Mario Balotelli put the visitors ahead. The Italian was later hauled down by Johnny Evans, who was duly sent off. Balotelli quickly made it 2-0, and

it began to look embarrassing for the champions when Sergio Aguero scored a third. Darren Fletcher pulled one back with ten minutes left, and the home fans suddenly started to believe in a comeback. Instead, City turned on the style to score three quick-fire goals and complete their rivals' worst home defeat since 1955.

LIVERPOOL 3-2 MANCHESTER CITY
Date: April 13, 2014 Venue: Anfield
Attendance: 44,601

8

On the day Anfield marked the 25th anniversary of Hillsborough, Liverpool took a huge step toward the title with a tenth successive win.

Brendan Rodgers' side stunned their opponents with a first-half onslaught topped by goals from Raheem Sterling and Martin Škrtel, but then allowed David Silva to level matters after the break with a close-range finish and a deflected equaliser. The

pendulum swung back Liverpool's way though, when Philippe Coutinho gobbled up Vincent Kompany's sliced clearance to score.

Liverpool held on for a huge victory, with Steven Gerrard wiping away his tears in a post-match huddle to demand his team-mates not let the League trophy slip away. Alas, they did just that.

57

7

"Kanu believe it!" bellowed Sky commentator Martin Tyler as the Arsenal striker's late hat-trick turned the game on its head at Stamford Bridge. After headed goals from Norwegian Tore Andre Flo and Romanian Dan Petrescu had given Chelsea the lead, Kanu pulled two back for the Gunners in the final 15 minutes, first prodding home from close range before screwing an effort past Ed de Goey in goal for the Blues. Nobody could have predicted what would happen next, though. The mercurial Nigerian broke free in injury-time, striding past the onrushing De Goey by the corner flag and curling home from the tightest of angles to complete a dramatic comeback for the Gunners.

CHELSEA 2-3 ARSENAL
Date: October 23, 1999
Venue: Stamford Bridge Attendance: 34,958

NEWCASTLE 5-0 MANCHESTER UNITED

Date: October 20, 1996 Venue: St. James' Park
Attendance: 36,579

Any Manchester United defeat is remembered by fans of the winning team, but this loss suffered by the double winners was so glorious in its magnitude, so unexpected and so emphatic, that it was celebrated far more widely than just on Tyneside.

Darren Peacock scored the first, his header crossing the line despite the protestations of Peter Schmeichel. David Ginola's outrageous second set the tone, while Les Ferdinand and Alan Shearer doubled the lead after the break and made Magpies fans

believe things couldn't get any better. How wrong they were, as Philippe Albert sealed the deal with a deft 25-yard lob over a stranded Schmeichel – not bad for a central defender.

5

Although Arsenal would go on to win the title in 1997-98, it wasn't all plain sailing. The Gunners endured a stuttering start, including this classic draw at Filbert Street. Dennis Bergkamp was the star of the show, putting the visitors 2-0 up after an hour. Arsenal seemed untroubled until Emile Heskey pulled one back late on, before Matt Elliot equalised in the 93rd minute. Bergkamp wasn't done, though, finding time to score one of the greatest ever Premier League goals. Bringing down a long David Platt pass over his shoulder, he flicked the ball inside Matt Elliott with his next touch before steadying himself and curling a shot past Kasey Keller for his hat-trick.

But this still wasn't the end of the action. The match endured long enough for Steve Walsh to head home the latest of levellers to send Filbert Street into delirium and earn Leicester a point.

4

Theo Walcott and Johan Djourou put Arsenal two up before the fourth minute at St. James' Park, before Robin van Persie grabbed two for himself to make it 4-0. It looked all over, but pity the disgruntled fans who left at the interval.

Two penalties from Barton and a Leon Best strike gave Newcastle a chance, with 10-man Arsenal rocking after Abou Diaby's red card. And then it came, a truly magnificent left-footed volley from the most unlikely of sources, Cheick Tiote. The Ivorian, as stunned as anyone to see the net ripple, ran halfway down the pitch in wild celebration – a jubilance shared by Newcastle's stunned supporters.

NEWCASTLE 4-4 ARSENAL
Date: February 5, 2011
Venue: St. James' Park
Attendance: 51,561

3

TOTTENHAM 3-5 MANCHESTER UNITED
Date: September 29, 2001
Venue: White Hart Lane Attendance: 36,038

Rarely has that old cliché 'a game of two halves' been a more appropriate way to describe a match than this momentous Manchester United fightback. Spurs romped into a 3-0 half-time lead thanks to goals from Dean Richards, Les Ferdinand and Christian Ziege, but Alex Ferguson worked his magic in the champions' dressing room during the break and United returned for the second half like a wounded animal.

Andy Cole scored within a minute of the restart and from that moment the tide turned, as Laurent Blanc, Ruud van Nistelrooy, Juan Sebastian Veron and David Beckham transformed what should have been a day of ecstasy for Tottenham into one of complete and utter agony.

61

LIVERPOOL 4-3 NEWCASTLE

Date: April 3, 1996 Venue: Anfield Attendance: 40,751

Both Liverpool and Newcastle were pushing Manchester United for the title, with the visitors knowing a win would take them level on points with the leaders.

Robbie Fowler gave the Reds an early lead, only for Les Ferdinand and David Ginola to quickly strike back. Fowler's second drew Liverpool level, but Faustino Asprilla soon edged Newcastle back in front. Stan Collymore popped up with another equaliser, and from then on both teams went hell for leather looking for a winner. It was Liverpool – and Collymore – who got it, prompting Magpies boss Kevin Keegan to slump forward in the dugout and provide one of the Premier League's most iconic images.

1

Sitting at the top of the Premier League at kick-off on the final day, all Manchester City had to do was beat QPR to win the title.

A tense first half got nervier when Wayne Rooney put title rivals Manchester United ahead at Sunderland, and although Pablo Zabaleta scored soon after, Djibril Cisse's equaliser early in the second period ramped up the blood pressure. Red-carded Joey Barton then tried to take some City players with him, before Jamie Mackie put the Hoops into an unlikely 66th-minute lead.

City entered the five minutes' added time 2-1 down, but Edin Džeko's leveller gave them hope. Three minutes later, Mario Balotelli's first assist of the season was smashed home by Sergio Aguero. Martin Tyler went berserk, and City were champions at the death.

MANCHESTER CITY 3-2 QPR
Date: May 13, 2012 Venue: The Etihad Attendance: 48,000

THE PREMIER LEAGUE'S
TOP 50
GOALSCORERS OF ALL TIME

Goals win football matches, which is why goalscorers are held in such high regard at any club. Since the Premier League's inaugural season in 1992-93, there have been a whole host of net-busters who have lit up the League. Here, we pay tribute to the best of them with a countdown of the Top 50 Premier League Scorers of All Time.

49=
DANIEL STURRIDGE
ENGLAND

2007-present
PL Goals: 74
PL Games: 200
PL Clubs: Man. City, Chelsea, Bolton, Liverpool

If it hadn't been for a succession of injuries and a frustrating start to his career, Sturridge would doubtless be much higher up this list. The Liverpool striker is one of the best one-on-one finishers in the Premier League, and when he's fully fit and on form, there aren't many better strikers in the Premier League.

49=
GABRIEL AGBONLAHOR
ENGLAND

2005-2017
PL Goals: 74
PL Games: 322
PL Clubs: Aston Villa

Local lad and one-club stalwart Agbonlahor enjoyed 11 seasons in the Premier League. He wasn't the most prolific striker, only hitting double figures in three seasons during a golden period from 2007 to 2010, but his pace, directness and work ethic for the team was invaluable to the Villans.

48
OLIVIER GIROUD
FRANCE

2012-present
PL Goals: 76
PL Games: 193
PL Clubs: Arsenal, Chelsea

After just six years in the Premier League and the fact he's not always been first choice at either Arsenal or Chelsea, the Frenchman has done pretty well to break into the top 50. To Giroud's credit, he's hit double figures every season, and with only 177 appearances, his strike rate of nearly a goal every other game is one most strikers would envy.

47
TONY COTTEE
ENGLAND

1992-2000
PL Goals: 78
PL Games: 220
PL Clubs: Everton, West Ham, Leicester

If the Premier League had been formed when Tony Cottee started his career, the striker would be second on this list of top goalscorers! Cottee's career began in 1982, ten years before the start of the PL, and in that time he scored 136 League goals for West Ham and Everton, before another 78 from 1992 onwards.

46
GARY SPEED
WALES

1992-2008
PL Goals: 80
PL Games: 535
PL Clubs: Leeds, Everton, Newcastle, Bolton

The Wales legend is the first midfielder in the list of top 50 goalscorers. His career spanned an incredible 22 seasons, with 16 of those coming in the Premier League. During that time Speed amassed 535 appearances, the fifth highest in PL history, and also scored in every one of his 16 seasons in the top flight.

45
CRAIG BELLAMY
WALES

2000-14
PL Goals: 81
PL Games: 294
PL Clubs: Coventry, Newcastle, Blackburn, Liverpool, West Ham, Man. City, Liverpool, Cardiff

Bellamy started his career at Norwich, before moving to Premier League side Coventry in 2000. Blessed with pace, tenacity and an eye for the goal, he was snapped up by Newcastle after just one season, and this set the tone for his career. In all, the striker scored for seven Premier League clubs, which is still a record.

43=
KEVIN CAMPBELL
ENGLAND

1992-2006
PL Goals: 83
PL Games: 325
PL Clubs: Arsenal, Nottingham Forest, Everton, West Brom

Campbell played for 14 seasons in the Premier League, scoring 83 goals from 325 games. His average of a goal every 3.9 games wasn't prolific, and he only hit double figures in three of those seasons, but Campbell was highly regarded wherever he played because of his work ethic, desire and ability to bring others into the game.

43=
CHRIS SUTTON
ENGLAND

1992-2007
PL Goals: 83
PL Games: 255
PL Clubs: Norwich, Blackburn, Chelsea, Birmingham, Aston Villa

After hitting 25 goals for Norwich in the 1993-94 season, Sutton was snapped up by Blackburn for a British record £5 million fee to play alongside Alan Shearer. Sutton – and the partnership – blossomed instantly, and Sutton's 15 goals helped Blackburn win the title that season. Spells at Chelsea, Birmingham and Aston Villa followed, but he will be remembered most for the SAS partnership with Shearer.

41=
CARLOS TEVEZ
ARGENTINA
2006-13
PL Goals: 84
PL Games: 202
PL Clubs: West Ham,
Man. United, Man. City

When Tevez moved to West Ham in 2006 it initially looked like a bad move – the striker didn't score until March. But then he hit seven goals in his last ten games to earn a move to Man. United, where he won two titles alongside Rooney and Ronaldo. He courted controversy again by moving to rivals City in 2009, where he enjoyed his best goals return, averaging a goal in less than two games.

41=
CRISTIANO RONALDO
PORTUGAL
2003-09
PL Goals: 84
PL Games: 196
PL Clubs: Man. United

When Ronaldo joined United he was primarily a winger and creator, and this was reflected in a return of just 18 goals in his first three seasons. Alex Ferguson then allowed him more freedom to roam and he hit 66 goals in his next three years at Old Trafford, equalling Alan Shearer's then-record of 31 goals in a 38-game season.

39=
LOUIS SAHA
FRANCE
1998-2013
PL Goals: 85
PL Games: 289
PL Clubs: Newcastle, Fulham, Man. United, Everton, Tottenham, Sunderland
Saha started his Premier League career at Newcastle, where he scored once in 11 games, but it was at Fulham where he caught the eye. He hit 13 goals in 21 games in 2003-04 to earn a move to Man. United, and though he only hit double figures once after that – in 2009-10 at Everton – he still scored an impressive 85 Premier League goals.

38
DENNIS BERGKAMP
HOLLAND
1995-2006
PL Goals: 87
PL Games: 315
PL Clubs: Arsenal
Bergkamp joined Arsenal from Inter Milan in 1995 and became one of the finest players of the era. Although not a prolific goalscorer, he hit double figures in his first four seasons at the club and produced 87 goals and 94 assists in 315 appearances. His partnership with Ian Wright won the title for Arsenal in 1998 and his subsequent pairing with Thierry Henry led to more wins in 2002, and the Invincibles year of 2004.

39=
FERNANDO TORRES
SPAIN
2007-16
PL Goals: 85
PL Games: 212
PL Clubs: Liverpool, Chelsea
Rarely has a deadline-day transfer drawn so stark a line through a career. Before his move to Chelsea in 2011 Torres was a prolific marksman, but after it he was anything but. In his first three years with Liverpool he was a phenomenon, hitting 56 Premier League goals. But after joining Chelsea he only scored another 20 in six years, with a succession of injuries blighting a Premier League career that could have been one of the best around.

37
KEVIN DAVIES
ENGLAND
1996-2012
PL Goals: 88
PL Games: 444
PL Clubs: Southampton, Blackburn, Bolton
Davies joined Southampton from Chesterfield as a 19-year-old and enjoyed a 16-year career in the Premier League. Another striker who could never be considered prolific – only reaching double figures in the 2008-09 season with Bolton – he was nevertheless an integral part of a Premier League Wanderers side for nine years and won an England cap in 2010.

35=
OLE GUNNAR SOLSKJAER
NORWAY
1996-2008
PL Goals: 91
PL Games: 235
PL Clubs: Man. United

Nicknamed the 'Baby-Faced Assassin', Solskjaer was regarded as something of a super sub: a third of Ole's League appearances were off the bench, meaning he impressively found the net once in every 150 minutes. Four strikes as a sub away at Nottingham Forest in 1999 was perhaps his greatest Premier League performance.

35=
JAMES BEATTIE
ENGLAND
1995-2011
PL Goals: 91
PL Games: 331
PL Clubs: Blackburn, Southampton, Everton, Stoke, Blackpool (loan)

After coming through the ranks at Blackburn, Beattie made his name at Southampton, where he scored double figures in four consecutive seasons between 2000-01 and 2003-04, hitting 23 in 2002-03. He won a total of five England caps and also enjoyed spells in the Premier League at Everton, Stoke and Blackpool.

33=
MARK VIDUKA
AUSTRALIA
2000-09
PL Goals: 92
PL Games: 240
PL Clubs: Leeds, Middlesbrough, Newcastle

Viduka joined Leeds from Celtic in 2000 for a fee of £6 million and had an immediate impact, scoring all four goals in a 4-3 win over Liverpool. He notched double figures in all four seasons at Elland Road before moving to Middlesbrough, where he played a vital role in their march to the Europa League final in 2006. A spell at Newcastle followed, but he could never recreate the glory.

33=
KEVIN PHILLIPS
ENGLAND
1999-2014
PL Goals: 92
PL Games: 263
PL Clubs: Sunderland, Southampton, Aston Villa, Birmingham, Crystal Palace

Phillips only made his Premier League debut in 1999 with Sunderland but scored an incredible 30 goals in his first season. He won the Premier League Golden Boot and the European Golden Shoe in the process, and is still the only Englishman to have won the latter. In 2003 the striker moved to Southampton before brief spells at Aston Villa, Birmingham and Crystal Palace in the Premier League.

30=
YAKUBU
NIGERIA
2003-12
PL Goals: 95
PL Games: 252
PL Clubs: Portsmouth, Middlesbrough, Everton, Blackburn

The Nigeria striker burst on to the Premier League scene with newly-promoted Portsmouth in 2003-04 and hit 28 goals in his first two seasons. That led to a move to Middlesbrough, where he hit double figures in both of his seasons there before Everton came calling. Following a great first campaign at Goodison Park he struggled with form and injuries and moved to Blackburn in 2011-12, where he hit an impressive 17 goals in 30 games.

32
DIMITAR BERBATOV
BULGARIA
2006-14
PL Goals: 94
PL Games: 229
PL Clubs: Tottenham, Man. United, Fulham

Despite featuring in the 2002 Champions League Final for Bayer Leverkusen, Berbatov was relatively unknown when he joined Spurs in 2006, but his laidback style and mastery of a football soon had Premier League fans taking notice. A £30 million move to Man. United followed, and in 2010-11 he hit a personal best of 20 goals as United won the title. He moved to Fulham in 2012 and scored 15 goals in his first season, including some absolute worldies.

30=
RUUD VAN NISTELROOY
HOLLAND
2001-06
PL Goals: 95
PL Games: 150
PL Clubs: Man. United

Few players enjoy their best years after a cruciate knee ligament injury, but Van Nistelrooy was one of them. He was named PFA Players' Player of the Year after his first campaign at Old Trafford and bagged the Premier League Golden Boot a year later, hitting 25 goals in the League and 44 overall. His goals-per-game ratio was superb but, surprisingly, the striker won only one League title in five seasons with the Red Devils.

29
EMMANUEL ADEBAYOR
TOGO
2005-16
PL Goals: 97
PL Games: 242
PL Clubs: Arsenal, Man. City, Tottenham, Crystal Palace

The Togo frontman netted 24 league goals for the Gunners in 2007-08 before moving to Man. City the following season, where he hit 14 goals in his first year at the Etihad. Adebayor then moved to Tottenham on loan in 2011 and scored 17 in his debut campaign for Spurs, but couldn't reproduce that kind of form after joining them permanently.

28
MATT LE TISSIER
ENGLAND
1992-2002
PL Goals: 100
PL Games: 270
PL Clubs: Southampton

Matt Le Tissier is arguably the finest player ever to pull on a Saints shirt. Blessed with an incredible touch, great skill and mastery of a football, he could also score goals others can only dream of. He scored 40 times in his first two Premier League seasons and 90 in his first six years, scoring double figures in five of them. He was also a superb penalty taker, and converted 24 in his total of 100 goals.

27
ROMELU LUKAKU
BELGIUM
2011-present
PL Goals: 101
PL Games: 220
PL Clubs: Chelsea, West Brom (loan), Everton, Man. United

Lukaku joined Chelsea in 2011 with an impressive reputation, having scored 41 goals for Anderlecht by the time he was 18. Despite Chelsea paying £17 million, he only started one League game before being loaned out to West Brom and then Everton, scoring 17 goals for the Baggies and 15 in his year at Goodison Park. He joined Everton in a permanent deal in 2014 and in an inconsistent team, scored 53 goals in three campaigns. That led to a £75 million switch to Man. United to be reunited with Jose Mourinho, the manager who sold him at Chelsea, where he hit 16 goals in his first Premier League season.

26
DIDIER DROGBA
IVORY COAST
2004-15
PL Goals: 104
PL Games: 254
PL Clubs: Chelsea

Drogba struggled in his first first few months in the Premier League, but the Ivory Coast star turned things around to become a legend. A powerhouse in the Blues' back-to-back title victories of 2004-05 and 2005-06, he won the Golden Boot a year later before repeating the feat with 29 goals in 2009-10. After spells in China and Turkey, he returned to Chelsea to claim a fourth title in 2015 and is the only African to hit 100 Premier League goals.

25
DARREN BENT
ENGLAND
2001-15
PL Goals: 106
PL Games: 276
PL Clubs: Ipswich, Charlton, Tottenham, Sunderland, Aston Villa, Fulham (loan)

Bent started his Premier League career at Ipswich, where his pace and eye for goal quickly alerted other clubs. He joined Charlton, where he scored in his first four Premier League games and hit double figures in his first two seasons at the club. A £16.5 million move to Tottenham followed, and despite finishing as the club's top scorer in 2008-09 he was sold to Sunderland, where he hit an impressive 24 Premier League goals in his first season. He joined Aston Villa for £24 million in 2010 but failed to hit double figures, which makes his goals per game ratio even more impressive.

24
PAUL SCHOLES
ENGLAND
1994-2013
PL Goals: 107
PL Games: 499
PL Clubs: Man. United

It is testament to Scholes' longevity as a player, rather than his goalscoring prowess, that sees the midfielder so high in the list of top scorers. Indeed, the Man. United legend only reached double figures twice, in 1995-96 and 2002-03, in a Premier League career that spanned 19 seasons. But Scholes' role wasn't as a goalscorer – he was a creator, and a superb one at that. The goals that he did score were often sensational, displaying technique and skill rarely seen in the Premier League.

22=
HARRY KANE
ENGLAND
2012-present
PL Goals: 108
PL Games: 153
PL Clubs: Tottenham

After spending the first few years of his career on loan, Kane burst on to the scene towards the end of the 2013-14 season, scoring on his first Premier League start against Sunderland and then finding the net in his next two games. From there, he hasn't looked back. He hit 21 league goals in 2014-15 and then won the Golden Boot the next two seasons with 25 and 29 goals respectively as Spurs finished third and second. He bettered both totals by hitting 30 Premier League strikes in 2017-18 but missed out on a third consecutive Golden Boot thanks to Mo Salah's incredible season. Despite that, the Tottenham striker has the best goals-per-game ratio of anyone on this list, netting on average every 1.42 games.

22=
PETER CROUCH
ENGLAND
2001-18
PL Goals: 108
PL Games: 462
PL Clubs: Aston Villa, Southampton, Liverpool, Portsmouth, Tottenham, Stoke

At 6ft 7ins tall, it maybe shouldn't come as a surprise that Crouch's 51 goals scored with his head is a Premier League record, but to define him by his heading ability would do him a disservice. During his 18 seasons in the Premier League he has impressed with good feet, a deft touch and an ability to score all types of goals. His goal ratio might not be up there with the best, but Crouch will still be remembered.

21
RYAN GIGGS
WALES
1992-2014
PL Goals: 109
PL Games: 632
PL Clubs: Man. United

Giggs is the only player to have played in the first 22 seasons of the Premier League and the only to have scored in the first 21, which is a remarkable achievement. Like team-mate Paul Scholes, he was more of a provider than goalscorer and on the list because of his longevity, Giggs could nevertheless score some stunning goals. He hit double figures in two seasons, 1993-94 and 1995-95, and was capable of scoring absolute stunners, beating several players to score to free-kicks and long-range efforts.

20
EMILE HESKEY
ENGLAND
1994-2012
PL Goals: 110
PL Games: 516
PL Clubs: Leicester, Liverpool, Birmingham, Wigan, Aston Villa

Often derided for his goalscoring, Heskey still scored an impressive 110 Premier League goals in a career that took in Leicester, Liverpool, Birmingham, Wigan and Aston Villa. Quick, strong and powerful, the striker also worked tirelessly, often occupying defenders to allow his strike partners to benefit — just ask Tony Cottee and Michael Owen.

19
DION DUBLIN
ENGLAND
1992-2004
PL Goals: 111
PL Games: 312
PL Clubs: Man. United, Coventry, Aston Villa

The big striker joined Man. United from Cambridge in 1992 and played seven times before suffering a broken leg. By the time he retuned to fitness United had signed Eric Cantona, so opportunities were limited; in 1994 Dublin moved to Coventry. There he hit double figures in all four seasons at the club and was the Premier League's joint top scorer in 1997-98 with 18 goals, which was all the more impressive in a team that finished 11th. The big, powerful hitman then moved to Aston Villa and spent six seasons at Villa Park, hitting double figures in three of those seasons.

18
IAN WRIGHT
ENGLAND
1992-99
PL Goals: 113
PL Games: 213
PL Clubs: Arsenal, West Ham

Wright joined Arsenal from Crystal Palace in 1991, the year before the Premier League began. He hit 15 league goals that season and was 28 years old when the first Premier League season kicked off, so his overall goal tally could have been much higher, had he had more years in the Premier League era. The striker beat Cliff Bastin's record of 178 goals for Arsenal in 1997, in just his seventh season with the club. His last act as a Gunner was to win the title in 1998 at the age of 34, before spending a season at West Ham. Quick, brave and determined, there were few better finishers than Wright.

17
STEVEN GERRARD
ENGLAND

1998-2015
PL Goals: 120
PL Games: 504
PL Clubs: Liverpool

As an all-action midfielder, goals were just a small part of Steven Gerrard's game, but the Liverpool star still scored an impressive 120 strikes in 504 games for the Reds. He hit double figures four times, including 16 strikes during the 2009-09 season when Liverpool finished runners-up to Man. United, and 13 in 2013-14, when they finished second to Man. City. A lover of shooting from distance and a brilliant free-kick taker, many of Gerrard's goals were spectacular, and a number were big goals in important matches.

16
DWIGHT YORKE
TRINIDAD & TOBAGO

1992-2009
PL Goals: 123
PL Games: 375
PL Clubs: Aston Villa, Man. United, Blackburn, Birmingham, Sunderland

After a relatively quiet start to his Premier League career, Dwight Yorke became Aston Villa's No.1 striker, hitting 17, 17 and 12 goals in the next three seasons to alert the attention of Man. United. At Old Trafford he formed a lethal partnership with Andy Cole, scoring 56 goals in 108 games as United won the Premier League for three consecutive seasons between 1999 and 2001. Yorke left United in 2002 for spells at Blackburn, Birmingham and Sunderland, but he could ever recreate the later years at Villa Park or the glory days at United.

15
NICOLAS ANELKA
FRANCE

1996-2014
PL Goals: 125
PL Games: 364
PL Clubs: Arsenal, Liverpool, Man. City, Bolton, Chelsea, West Brom

A title-winner at Arsenal when he was 19, the following campaign brought 17 goals and an ill-fated switch to Madrid. But Anelka moved back to England with Liverpool and Man. City before departing again for Fenerbahce. Sam Allardyce revived Anelka's career at Bolton and the French striker became the Premier League's top scorer with 19 for Chelsea in 2008-09, winning another title a year later. He and Tevez are the only two players on this list to earn a Winner'sMmedal with more than one team. After transferring to China, Anelka's final Premier League stint came at West Brom.

14
ROBBIE KEANE
REPUBLIC OF IRELAND

1999-2012
PL Goals: 126
PL Games: 349
PL Clubs: Coventry, Leeds, Tottenham, Liverpool, West Ham (loan), Aston Villa

Keane joined Coventry at the age of 19 for a fee of £6 million, which was then a British record for a teenager. After scoring 12 Premier League goals in his first season he was snapped up by Inter Milan, but things didn't go to plan in Italy and he returned to the Premier League with Leeds. The striker moved to Spurs in 2002 and found his form, scoring double figures in each of his six seasons at the club. An unsuccessful move to Liverpool followed before returning to Tottenham, before finally seeing out spells at Aston Villa and West Ham on loan.

11
ROBIN VAN PERSIE
HOLLAND
2004-15
PL Goals: 144
PL Games: 280
PL Clubs: Arsenal, Man. United

Alex Ferguson's final season in charge of Manchester United delivered the league crown, largely down to Van Persie's move from rivals Arsenal. The Dutchman hadn't won the League in eight campaigns in north London – he joined the club a couple of days after the end of the Invincibles season in 2004 – and injuries occasionally prevented him showing his full potential as he switched from a wideman to a striker. But the left-footer reached his peak at the age of 28, winning the Golden Boot with 30 efforts in his final season at the Emirates, before netting 26 times in his debut term at Old Trafford to help Fergie bid farewell with a 13th league title to his name.

13
JIMMY FLOYD HASSELBAINK
HOLLAND
1997-2007
PL Goals: 127
PL Games: 288
PL Clubs: Leeds, Chelsea, Middlesbrough, Charlton

Only three players have topped the Premier League scoring charts with more than one team – Robin van Persie, Alan Shearer and Hasselbaink. The powerful striker scored 18 times with Leeds, sharing the Golden Boot award with Michael Owen and Dwight Yorke in 1998-99 and, following a season with Atletico Madrid, he netted 23 times in 35 appearances for Chelsea in 2000-01. Possessing a rocket of a right foot, Jimmy helped a resurgent Blues finish second in 2004 before moves to Middlesbrough and Charlton.

12
SERGIO AGUERO
ARGENTINA
2011-present
PL Goals: 143
PL Games: 206
PL Clubs: Man. City

Only Harry Kane and Thierry Henry can rival the Man. City striker's goals-per-game ratio. The late, late strike against QPR that sealed City the title in 2012 was one of English football's most dramatic moments, and the goal came at the end of the first of seven full campaigns to date at City, with the 30-year-old hitting the 20-goal mark in four of those. Incredibly, Aguero has only made the PFA Team Of The Season once, in 2017-18.

10
TEDDY SHERINGHAM
ENGLAND
1992-2007
PL Goals: 146
PL Games: 418
PL Clubs: Nottingham Forest, Tottenham, Man. United, Portsmouth, West Ham

Sheringham hadn't won a major title before 1999, but helped the Red Devils to three League trophies in four seasons at Old Trafford, earning him the Footballer of the Year honour at the age of 34. He was top scorer in the first Premier League campaign after moving from Nottingham Forest to Tottenham in the early weeks of the season. Teddy later played for Portsmouth and West Ham, becoming the oldest scorer in the Premier League at the age of 40.

9
LES FERDINAND
ENGLAND
1992-2005
PL Goals: 149
PL Games: 351
PL Clubs: QPR, Newcastle, Tottenham, West Ham, Leicester, Bolton

No-one can boast a higher Premier League goal tally despite not scoring a single penalty. Sir Les didn't need any spot-kicks – he bagged 101 goals in the first five seasons of the Premier League, joining Newcastle United from Queens Park Rangers in 1995. Kevin Keegan's ill-fated title tilt proved the closest Ferdinand came to winning the League, but he continued to find the net at Spurs, West Ham and Leicester – where he scored 12 times in the season of his 37th birthday – before a stint with Bolton.

7
JERMAIN DEFOE
ENGLAND
1998-present
PL Goals: 162
PL Games: 492
PL Clubs: West Ham, Tottenham, Portsmouth, Sunderland, Bournemouth

A consistent goalscorer, Defoe has hit double figures in ten different Premier League seasons and is the only player to have netted five goals in one half, in Tottenham's 9-1 demolition of Wigan in 2009. He also holds the record for the most goals as a sub – 23 – including a screamer against Man. City in 2013 – and is one of the most respected strikers around.

8
MICHAEL OWEN
ENGLAND
1996-2013
PL Goals: 150
PL Games: 326
PL Clubs: Liverpool, Newcastle, Man. United, Stoke

Owen was just 18 and still in his first full season as a regular with Liverpool when he shared the Golden Boot in 1997-98. Not content with that, he repeated the feat a year later after becoming a hero for England at the World Cup thanks to that goal against Argentina. The speedy striker would go on to seal the Ballon d'Or in 2001 and posted double figures in each of his seven full seasons in the Liverpool first team. But moves to Real Madrid and Newcastle didn't work out as planned, and injury woes meant he was a bit-part player when he finally won a League title at Manchester United in 2011, before ending his career at Stoke.

6
ROBBIE FOWLER
ENGLAND
1992-2009
PL Goals: 163
PL Games: 379
PL Clubs: Liverpool, Leeds, Man. City, Blackburn

Fowler scored his first hat-trick against Southampton on his fifth league appearance, and his second against Arsenal on his 30th (the latter coming in just five first-half minutes). In the age of Shearer, Klinsmann and Wright, Fowler was the most clinical of all Premier League strikers. Then a knee ligament injury in 1996-97 stopped the goal poacher in his tracks, with Michael Owen pinching his place in the Reds' XI. Fowler eventually made his comeback, but had lost the explosiveness that once made him so feared by Premier League defences. Spells with Leeds and Man. City, and even an emotional return to Anfield in January 2006, failed to see the striker regularly recreate the old magic.

5
THIERRY HENRY
FRANCE
1999-2012
PL Goals: 175
PL Games: 258
PL Clubs: Arsenal

Henry may not have scored as many Premier League goals as Shearer, but he didn't play in as many matches – 258 to Shearer's 441 – and the ex-Arsenal man's goals-per-game ratio is actually better. The France international achieved this with a panache that made him both an Arsenal and Premier League icon. He found the net 24 times in 2001-02 to help the north Londoners win the title, following it with 24, 30, 25 and 27 in each of the next four seasons. No other player has ever hit more than 20 goals in five consecutive campaigns, and on four of those occasions he was Premier League top scorer. He made a brief return to London in January 2012 on loan, with the sole League strike of his second spell a last-minute winner away at Sunderland. While Shearer lifted the title just once, Henry was rarely away from the title race. His second crown, when he was the star of the Invincibles team of 2003-04 with 30 goals in 37 appearances, earned him Premier League immortality.

4
FRANK LAMPARD
ENGLAND
1995-2015
PL Goals: 177
PL Games: 609
PL Clubs: West Ham, Chelsea, Man. City

Put simply, Lampard's goal tally is nothing short of remarkable. He played his entire 20-year Premier League career as a midfielder but didn't score in his first two seasons, and then only hit 35 in his next six. But at Chelsea, he scored double figures in 11 consecutive Premier League seasons, including 22 in the 2009-10 campaign as Chelsea won the title and Lampard finished fifth in the list of top scorers.

3
ANDREW COLE
ENGLAND
1993-2008
PL Goals: 187
PL Games: 414
PL Clubs: Newcastle, Man. United, Blackburn, Fulham, Man. City, Portsmouth, Sunderland

It's incredible to think that Andy Cole scored nearly a fifth of entire Premier League goal tally in his first season in the Premier League but the Newcastle striker scored an astonishing 34 goals in 40 games for the Magpies, setting a new Premier League record in the process. In 1994 he moved to Man. United, where he partnered Eric Cantona, Dwight Yorke and Teddy Sheringham in a spell that saw him win five Premier League titles. Cole's pace, anticipation and cool head in front of goal saw him become a big favourite at Old Trafford, and though spells at Blackburn, Fulham, Man. City, Portsmouth and Sunderland wouldn't be as successful, his goal tally will rightly see him as one of the Premier League's great goalscorers.

1

ALAN SHEARER
ENGLAND
1992-2006
PL Goals: 260
PL Games: 441
PL Clubs: Blackburn, Newcastle

Quite simply, Alan Shearer is a phenomenon. After joining Blackburn for a British record £3 million in the summer of 1992, the next 14 seasons saw goal after goal after goal. He hit 16 in the 1992-93 season despite not starting a game after Boxing Day, and hit an incredible 31 goals from 40 games the following season despite not starting a game until September. He scored 34 goals – a joint Premier League record – in 1994-95 as Blackburn won the Premier League, and then became the only player to hit 30 goals or more in three consecutive seasons when he hit 31 goals in the 1995-95 campaign. Another British record move followed, to hometown club Newcastle, where he hit double figures in seven of his ten seasons and 148 in total. The only reason he didn't score more was due to a succession of injuries, meaning his overall goals haul could and would have been significantly higher. The Premier League has never witnessed a goalscoring machine quite like him.

2

WAYNE ROONEY
ENGLAND
2002-2018
PL Goals: 208
PL Games: 491
PL Clubs: Everton, Man. United

Rooney's stunner for Everton against Arsenal in October 2002, aged 16, was the first of what would prove to be an incredible 208 Premier League goals. Although not prolific in his two seasons at the Toffees, a superb showing for England at Euro 2004 led Alex Ferguson to pay £30 million for the striker. There, he scored double figures in 12 of his 14 seasons at the club, winning five Premier League titles and the PFA Players' Player of the Year prize in 2010. The striker made an emotional move back to boyhood club Everton in 2017-18 and scored ten Premier League goals. He has also weighed in with over 100 assists, a tally only bettered by Ryan Giggs, Cesc Fabregas and Frank Lampard.

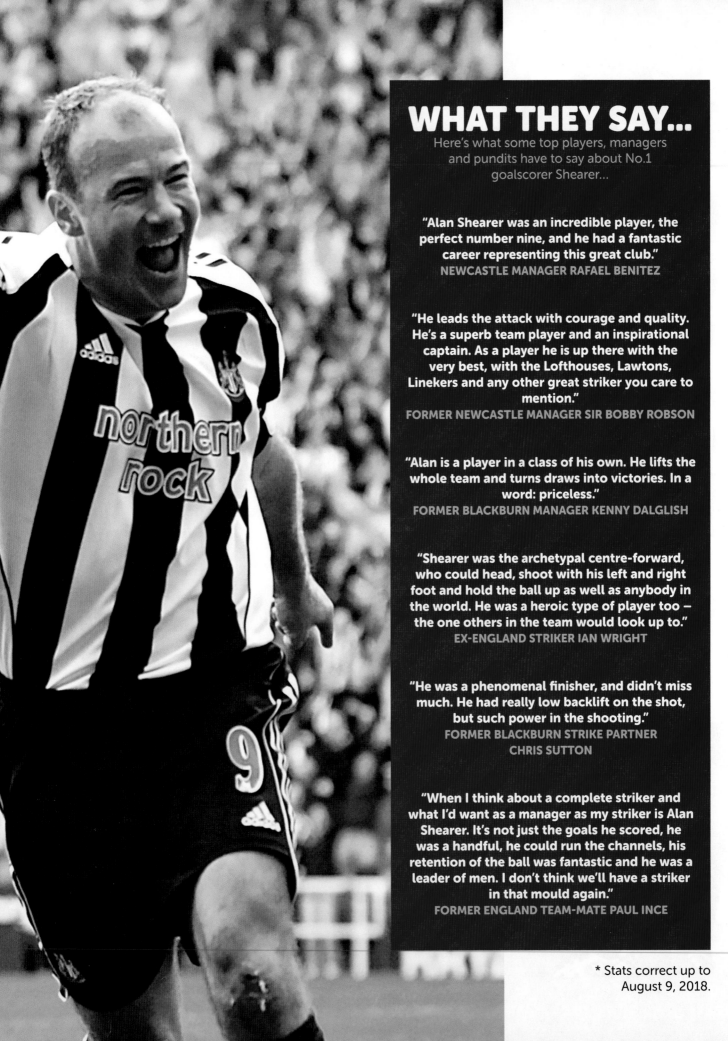

WHAT THEY SAY...

Here's what some top players, managers and pundits have to say about No.1 goalscorer Shearer...

"Alan Shearer was an incredible player, the perfect number nine, and he had a fantastic career representing this great club."
NEWCASTLE MANAGER RAFAEL BENITEZ

"He leads the attack with courage and quality. He's a superb team player and an inspirational captain. As a player he is up there with the very best, with the Lofthouses, Lawtons, Linekers and any other great striker you care to mention."
FORMER NEWCASTLE MANAGER SIR BOBBY ROBSON

"Alan is a player in a class of his own. He lifts the whole team and turns draws into victories. In a word: priceless."
FORMER BLACKBURN MANAGER KENNY DALGLISH

"Shearer was the archetypal centre-forward, who could head, shoot with his left and right foot and hold the ball up as well as anybody in the world. He was a heroic type of player too — the one others in the team would look up to."
EX-ENGLAND STRIKER IAN WRIGHT

"He was a phenomenal finisher, and didn't miss much. He had really low backlift on the shot, but such power in the shooting."
FORMER BLACKBURN STRIKE PARTNER CHRIS SUTTON

"When I think about a complete striker and what I'd want as a manager as my striker is Alan Shearer. It's not just the goals he scored, he was a handful, he could run the channels, his retention of the ball was fantastic and he was a leader of men. I don't think we'll have a striker in that mould again."
FORMER ENGLAND TEAM-MATE PAUL INCE

* Stats correct up to August 9, 2018.

THE BEST PREMIER LEAGUE KITS EVER

The launch of your new team's kit is usually met with more than a little trepidation. For every great kit, there's the abomination you instantly hated and convinced yourself it would be the sole reason your team were relegated that season. Some teams are luckier than others, some eras were better than others. But here are some of the greatest kits ever to grace the Premier League, followed by those that should never have seen the light of day...

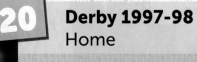

20 Derby 1997-98
Home

For some reason, shirts became incredibly baggy in the late '90s. However, the Rams' smart Puma-made white effort was one of the few that looked good, particularly when modelled by Paolo Wanchope – a mass of limbs and skill, wrapped in a shirt the size of a beach windbreak.

18 Everton 2015-16
Home

A little turret and a couple of elephants can only make a football shirt better, and while all Umbro's efforts have been decent, last season's version was possibly the best, making Leighton Baines look every inch the mod idol.

19 Liverpool 1992-93
Away

The Premier League hasn't seen enough green kits since it began. This Liverpool away kit from the first season is a devilishly handsome shade of green, is simple and bold. It shouts "Check me out!" and you have to admire adidas' bravado in plastering those three massive stripes on the shoulder.

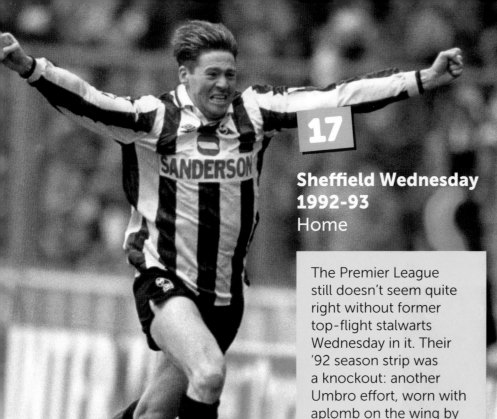

17
Sheffield Wednesday 1992-93
Home

The Premier League still doesn't seem quite right without former top-flight stalwarts Wednesday in it. Their '92 season strip was a knockout: another Umbro effort, worn with aplomb on the wing by Chris Waddle.

16
Man. City 1994-95
Away

City may have been a shambles on the pitch, but their Umbro tops were always great. The understated Cambridge blue and the pinstriped white away versions particularly stood out, and were donned on lads mag covers by Liam and Noel Gallagher – making the 'Brother' sponsor seem even more apt.

15
Tottenham 1993-95
Home

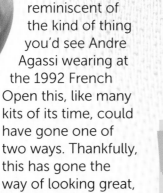

With a daring shoulder design reminiscent of the kind of thing you'd see Andre Agassi wearing at the 1992 French Open this, like many kits of its time, could have gone one of two ways. Thankfully, this has gone the way of looking great, and has even aged pretty well too.

14
Coventry 1996-97
Home

Coventry's kits over the years have arguably been some of the worst of any club anywhere on earth, but this Le Coq Sportif effort was the exception to the rule – sky blue/dark blue combo worn beautifully by the likes of Peter Ndlovu.

13
Wimbledon 1994-95
Home

Wimbledon never did anything by the book, and didn't even bother having a kit supplier in this season – instead getting 'The Crazy Gang' embroidered over the heart. An unusual combo of dark blue and yellow trim, it's the only kit you'd want an opponent to be wearing as they kicked you all over the park.

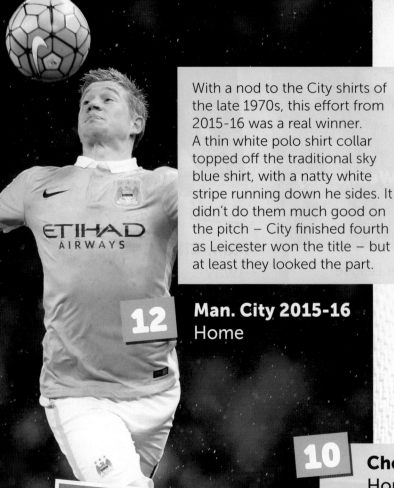

With a nod to the City shirts of the late 1970s, this effort from 2015-16 was a real winner. A thin white polo shirt collar topped off the traditional sky blue shirt, with a natty white stripe running down he sides. It didn't do them much good on the pitch – City finished fourth as Leicester won the title – but at least they looked the part.

12 Man. City 2015-16
Home

11 West Brom 2016-17
Home

Baggies' kits looked amazing in the 60's and '70s, before running a load of awfulness through much of the next three decades. But 2016-17's effort was genuinely stunning: with UK-K8.com's Chinese lettering combining perfectly with the traditional old stripes, it looked like it was beamed down from space (in a good way).

10 Chelsea 2001-03
Home

Chelsea's suppliers have never had trouble making great-looking kits: white on royal blue is always cracking, and even the current adidas kit is pretty special. But this one was deeply simple in the best possible way, with a clean design and the marvellous old Chelsea lion badge – which all big cat enthusiasts agree should never have been changed.

9 Tottenham 1997-99
Home

David Ginola can't be seen in any old tat – and the French idol looked impeccable in this glorious Tottenham top with its minimalist design and retro collar. The German duo of adidas and Holsten was also apt for the era of Jurgen Klinsmann.

8 Liverpool 2013-14
Home

Liverpool had some of the best kits in the '60s, '70s and '80s – simple, bold and striking – before hitting the skids through much of the Premier League era, both on the pitch and in the designer's studio. But the 2013-14 model was the best effort: a tip of the hat to the side's much-told history without wallowing in nostalgia.

7
Blackburn 1994-95
Home

It's hard to get a Blackburn kit wrong: simple blue and white halves always look terrific, and the year they won the Premier League title also coincided with one of their most beautiful shirts, a natty effort that somehow even a McEwan's logo couldn't spoil.

6
Leeds 2000-02
Home

5
West Ham 1999-01
Home

The best claret 'n' blue shirt ever made: a rare Fila venture into the field of making UK kits, this none-more-London combo of classic colours and Dr Martens' sponsor logo looked a treat on the back of crazy genius Paolo Di Canio.

The shirt that harks back to the time Leeds were involved in the title races, unforgettable Champions League nights at Elland Road, and United's vibrant, young team. Some might say the shirt's a bit plain but the beauty is in its simplicity; and the yellow and blue trim on the neck and sleeves works well. Hell, even the Strongbow sponsorship looks good, which is an achievement in itself.

4
Arsenal 2005-06
Home

An opinion-divider (some felt Arsenal should always wear a proper red), the 'currant' kit was brought in for sentimental reasons: the Gunners were leaving Highbury and decided to replicate the colour they'd worn in 1913, the year they moved in. Wrong or not, it looked great on Thierry and company.

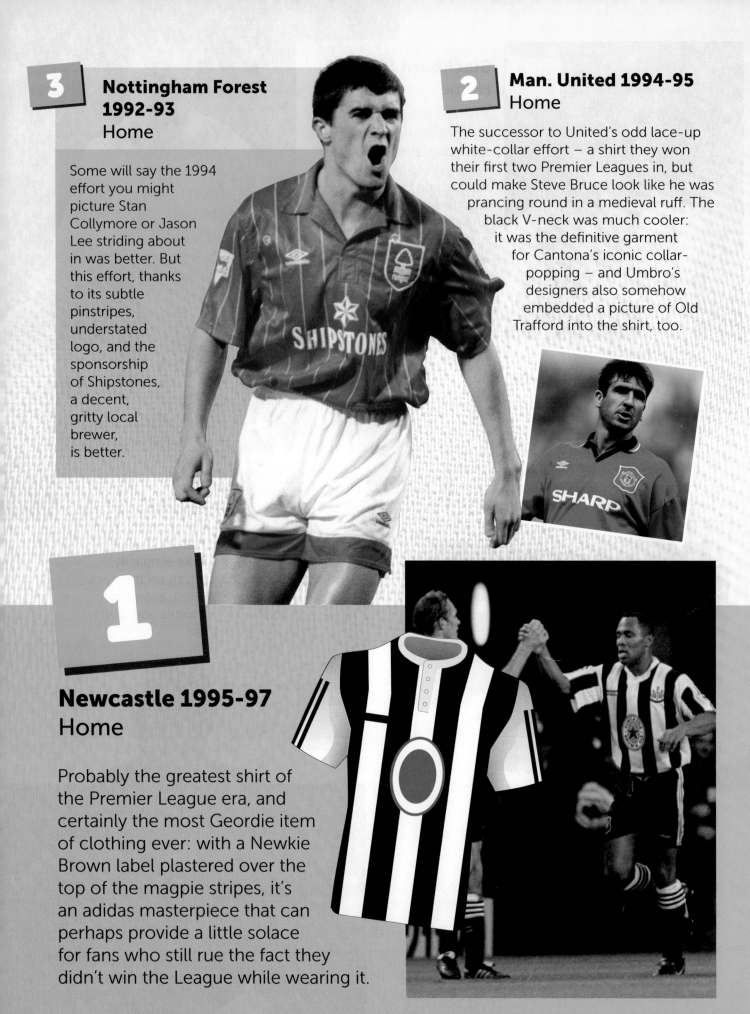

3 Nottingham Forest 1992-93
Home

Some will say the 1994 effort you might picture Stan Collymore or Jason Lee striding about in was better. But this effort, thanks to its subtle pinstripes, understated logo, and the sponsorship of Shipstones, a decent, gritty local brewer, is better.

2 Man. United 1994-95
Home

The successor to United's odd lace-up white-collar effort – a shirt they won their first two Premier Leagues in, but could make Steve Bruce look like he was prancing round in a medieval ruff. The black V-neck was much cooler: it was the definitive garment for Cantona's iconic collar-popping – and Umbro's designers also somehow embedded a picture of Old Trafford into the shirt, too.

1 Newcastle 1995-97
Home

Probably the greatest shirt of the Premier League era, and certainly the most Geordie item of clothing ever: with a Newkie Brown label plastered over the top of the magpie stripes, it's an adidas masterpiece that can perhaps provide a little solace for fans who still rue the fact they didn't win the League while wearing it.

...AND THE WORST

20 Tottenham 2009-10
Home

Spurs kits tend to be pretty solid – the ol' lily white and navy are a strong aesthetic pairing – but unnecessary yellow flanks and chest swipes pooped this shirt's party, while MANSION DOT COM CASINO & POKER was also a bit of a mouthful. Disappointing.

19 Man. United 1992-94
Third

United fans have used green and gold to great effect over recent years as part of their protests over the club's ownership, but back in '92 the club themselves happily embraced the colours to celebrate the 100-year-old Newton Heath design. While iconic, the shirt was pretty nasty, and mainly serves to remind you why they switched to red.

18 Chelsea 2007-08
Away

If Man. United couldn't see each other in their notorious grey jerseys, then there were no such issues for Jose Mourinho's (and from September, Avram Grant's) men in this season. With neon tops visible from space, the only issue here was working out who was a player and who was a fan, steward or errant lollipop lady.

17 Newcastle 1997-98
Away

While Chelsea once had to worry about clashing with stewards, the Newcastle team of 1997-98 had to worry about clashing with the referee. In fact, the man in black had to change his jersey during the Geordies' 4-1 away defeat to Leeds because their hideous, partly striped kit was so dark.

16 Middlesbrough 1996-97
Away

Nineties 'Boro were a lot of fun for several reasons: the Riverside, Fabrizio Ravanelli, Juninho, promotion, relegation, re-promotion and cup finals. They also sported some very fine red shirts during the period – but this Errea effort was a misstep, from the walloping BORO scrawled over the arm to the curious cross made out of your nan's decaying curtains.

15 Man. City 2008-09
Away

It's hard to imagine the likes of Aguero, De Bruyne and Mendy trotting out at the Etihad Stadium in the kind of orange kit that made Sunny Delight look entirely natural. But that's what Man. City were forced to sport before they became the multi-billion dollar superclub they are today.

Everton 2010-11
Away

There's nothing wrong with a nice bit of pink on a football shirt – Juventus have done it stylishly, and Palermo rock the electric shade week in, week out. But the Toffees' attempt was a rotting salmon, making Diniyar Bilyaletdinov, Phil Jagielka & co. look like 1980s mismatched socks.

 Coventry 1992-94
Away

Coventry City is renowned for producing perhaps the ugliest kit in English football history – the hideous chocolate-brown one of the late 70s. But they're also responsible for another top-flight monstrosity, namely this bizarre Jackson Pollock-inspired kit from 1992.

 Aston Villa 1993-95
Away

Aston Villa's sponsors in the mid-90s surely can't have been too pleased about the mismatched green, red and black combo of the club's away kit. Indeed, it's hard to imagine many fans wanting to tuck into a Muller corner after watching such an unappetising colour combo for 90 minutes.

 Huddersfield 2017-18
Third

Huddersfield Town haven't wasted any time in joining the pantheon of worst Premier League kits. The newly promoted side spent their first season in the top flight since 1972 saddled with a ghastly red-and-black 'electric hoops flash' kit similar to the one they wore in the early 90s.

 Fulham 2010-11
Third

Now the Fulham of 2010-11 could have actually got away with using Alex Ferguson's hilariously daft excuse. Indeed, their olive-green third kit, complete with gold trim, instantly made Clint Dempsey and his team blend into the pitch.

 Sunderland 2016-17
Third

Sunderland's kit makers appeared to take one look at Everton's monstrosity and ask 'how can we make it even more unsightly?' The answer was to offset the bright pink with purple stripes and migraine-inducing diagonal lines.

 Liverpool 2013-14
Away

Brendan Rodgers' men had a smashing season in 2013-14 – which was lucky, because they looked terrible on their travels. The top half of this one was reasonable, with standard enough red-on-white lines, but what was going on in the bottom half? A malfunctioning television?

 Liverpool 2013-14
Third

Astonishingly, Liverpool's white away kit from this season – quite comfortably one of the worst shirts of the Premier League era – wasn't even the worst away shirt the club had that term. An internal investigation leading to several sackings must surely have been undertaken at Warrior after this design was allowed to become reality.

Blackburn 1996-97
Away

While Blackburn's home kits have almost always been models of tasteful understatement, this away effort was genuinely upsetting. Its sprinkled black club crest collage, down one side and along a sleeve, made Colin Hendry and friends look like they'd succumbed to some sort of jaundicing tropical disease.

Norwich 1992-93
Home

This avant-garde take on the Canaries' famous yellow-and-green colours will always hold special memories for long-time Norwich City fans. It was the kit the likes of Chris Sutton and Robert Fleck wore during the glorious mid-90s phase in which they finished third in the Premier League and beat Bayern Munich in the UEFA Cup. But there's no getting away from the fact the team always looked like their kit room had been invaded by a flock of incontinent pigeons.

Man United 1992-93
Away

A kit that made even king of cool Eric Cantona look like an idiot, the whacking great club crest and peculiar black stripes were further proof that just because you can suddenly design such things, doesn't mean you should.

Tottenham 2006-07
Third

Chocolate brown also made an unwanted top-flight reappearance during the 2006-07 season, with Spurs being the guilty culprits. The North Londoners also added some gold into the mix for that extra chocolate-box touch.

Nottingham Forest 1995-97
Away

After becoming the first ever Premier League team to be relegated, Nottingham Forest seemed determined to leave a much longer-lasting impression when they bounced back for a brief three-year spell. And they certainly did that with an away kit which essentially looked like a bunch of toddlers had been given free rein with a marker pen.

Norwich 2015-16
Third

Let's make no bones about it, this 2015-16 third kit from repeat offenders Norwich is hideous. But not only is it an abomination on the eyes, it also combines the same colours as both the Canaries' home and away kits, so it's just as pointless as it is offensive, which takes some doing.

THE GREATEST PREMIER LEAGUE TEAMS OF ALL TIME

Over the years, the Premier League has seen a number of incredible players. But every now and then, a group of wonderful players are assembled in the same team, and those teams produce seasons that last long in the memory. Some might be full of flair and goals, others might be based around impenetrable defences, while others rip up the rule book completely to produce football that has never been seen previously. So here they are, the ten finest teams of the Premier League era.

2007-08

MAN. UNITED

This remarkable side had pretty much everything. Edwin van der Sar was back to his best in goal, while Rio Ferdinand and Nemanja Vidić were the best centre-back combination in Europe.

Further forward, Paul Scholes, Owen Hargreaves and Michael Carrick were three of the most intelligent of their generation, while the attacking trio of Cristiano Ronaldo, Carlos Tevez and Wayne Rooney rotated at will and caused havoc in opposition defences. Ronaldo, in particular, was unstoppable, and this campaign helped him win the Ballon d'Or.

The supporting cast were Park Ji-sung, Darren Fletcher and John O'Shea weren't the most fashionable players, but were intelligent, tactical options who helped nullify opponents. In truth, though, this United were a better European side than a Premier League side – they only beat Avram Grant's Chelsea side by two points.

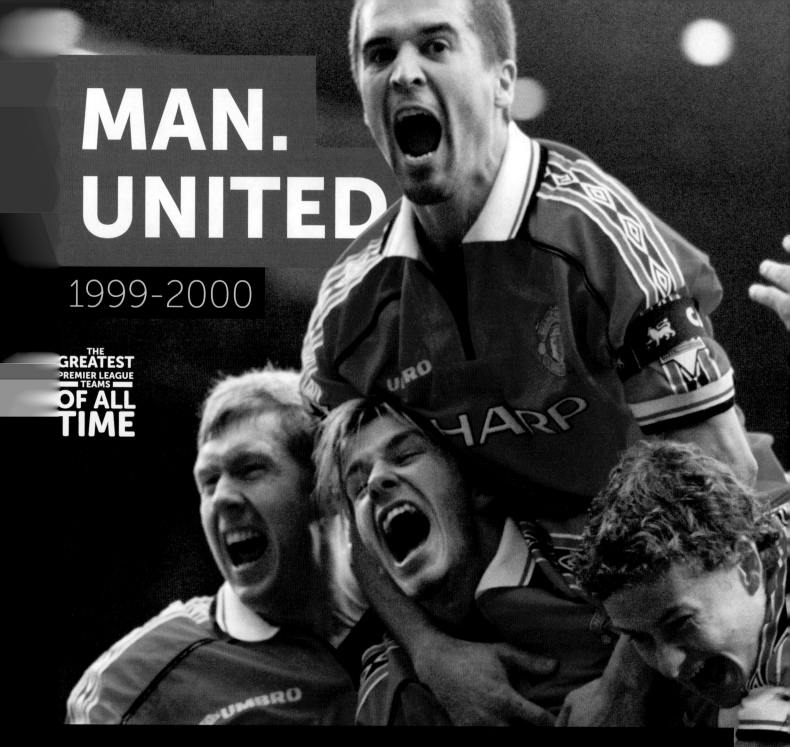

MAN. UNITED

1999-2000

THE GREATEST PREMIER LEAGUE TEAMS OF ALL TIME

It seems strange to include this side rather than the famous treble winners of the previous season – the 1998-99 side's achievements were clearly more memorable.

But in 1999-2000, Manchester United improved their points tally by 12 and scored 17 more goals. Whereas in 1998-99 they needed a final day comeback to sneak the title by a point, in 1999-2000 they won by 18.

It was largely the same team as the treble-winners: the best midfield quartet of the Premier League era in David Beckham, Paul Scholes, Roy Keane and Ryan Giggs. Further forward, the partnership of Andy Cole and Dwight Yorke backed up by super-subs Teddy Sheringham and Ole Gunnar Solskjaer. Mikael Silvestre provided extra pace at the back, and the only weakness was in goal, where Mark Bosnich proved an underwhelming replacement for Peter Schmeichel.

LEICESTER

Leicester's remarkable title victory was so unexpected th[at it] feels impossible to compare it to the big boys' successes [—] forget their underdog status and see the dominance of th[eir] title victory, claiming the title by an impressive ten points [and] only losing three times all season.

Claudio Ranieri's side ripped up the rulebook – whereas [the] others were obsessed with possession play, Leicester wer[e] almost pure counter-attackers. Jamie Vardy broke the Premier League record for scoring in consecutive games, Riyad Mahrez was the league's best player – capable of scoring, creating and assisting – while N'Golo Kanté was a revelation.

But more than anything this was a brilliant team, and amor[g] the best defensive units the Premier League has seen in th[e] second half of the season. When asked questions they alwa[ys] came up with the answers – pressing higher or going more direct with supersub Leonardo Ulloa. The most extraordina[ry] unlikely title winners, they're also among the best.

MAN. UNITED

Manchester United were serial title winners during the Premier League's early years, but this was their most dominant triumph of the 1990s: a formidable, consistent side that were top of the table after 40 of their 42 matches.

Tactically, it was considered a 4-4-2, although they were perhaps the first 4-2-3-1 Premier League side. Newcomer Roy Keane formed a terrifying midfield partnership with Paul Ince; both box-to-box midfielders rather than holders. Two of Lee Sharpe, Andrei Kanchelskis and Ryan Giggs provided pace out wide while up front, Eric Cantona orchestrated play behind a good old-fashioned target man, Mark Hughes.

The back four was barely ever broken up – Denis Irwin was ever-present, centre-back duo Steve Bruce and Gary Pallister missed one game each, Paul Parker just two. Peter Schmeichel was the League's best goalkeeper. No one stood a chance.

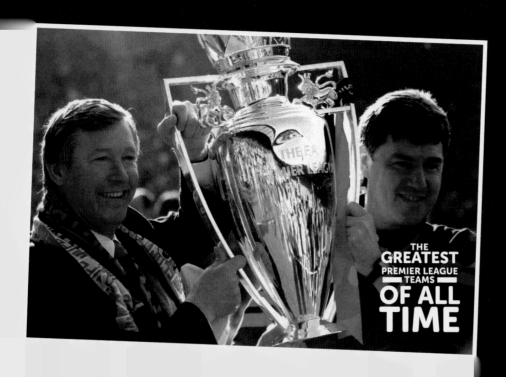

THE
GREATEST
PREMIER LEAGUE
TEAMS
OF ALL
TIME

Officially the greatest: by wins, goals, points, winning margin, goal difference and more.

Yes, this was a expensively assembled group of players, but then when has money ever guaranteed success? Man. City were a costly team in 2016-17 when they finished third, some 15 points behind champions Chelsea.

Pep Guardiola needed a second season to take this team to new heights, crafting a dominant side which swept all before them. Well, almost: Liverpool beat them, as did Man. United – their only two defeats – and then the Merseysiders did so again in the Champions League quarter-finals.

It's a blot on Man City's season, certainly, but really shouldn't detract from their domestic achievements over the course of an incredible campaign. They hit the magical 100-point mark with a glorious lob from Gabriel Jesus in the 94th minute of their final match of the season – and celebrated like they'd won the title all over again.

MAN. CITY

2017-18

THE GREATEST PREMIER LEAGUE TEAMS OF ALL TIME

THE ALL TIME PREMIER LEAGUE
RECORDS

When Man. City won the Premier League in 2017-18 they re-wrote the history books, breaking an incredible 11 records along the way. But there are still plenty they haven't beaten – yet – so in homage to Pep Guardiola's title winners, and to acknowledge those whose records still remain, here's a list of the all-time Premier League records.

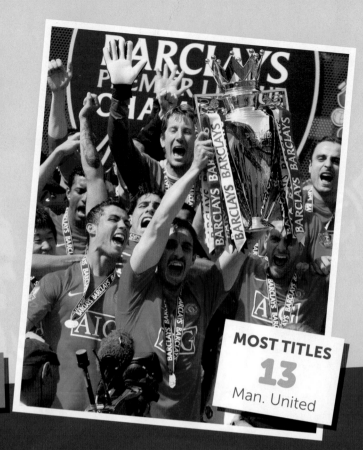

MOST TITLES
13
Man. United

CLUB RECORDS

MOST CONSECUTIVE TITLE WINS
3
Man. United
(1998-99, 1999-2000, 2000-01 & 2006-07, 2007-08, 2008-09)

FEWEST POINTS IN A SEASON
11
Derby (2007-08)

MOST CONSECUTIVE GAMES WITHOUT A WIN
32
Derby (2007-08)

BIGGEST TITLE-WINNING MARGIN
19 points
Man. City (2017-18)

MOST WINS IN A SEASON
32
Man. City (2017-18)

LONGEST UNBEATEN RUN
49 games
Arsenal
(7 May, 2003 to 24 October, 2004)

FEWEST WINS IN A SEASON
1
Derby (2007-08)

SMALLEST TITLE-WINNING MARGIN
0 points and 8 goals difference
Man. City (2011-12)

FEWEST DEFEATS IN A SEASON
0
Arsenal (2003-04)

MOST CONSECUTIVE WINS
18
Man. City
(2017-18) (26 August, 2017 to 27 December, 2017

MOST CONSECUTIVE HOME GAMES UNBEATEN
86
Chelsea
(March 20, 2004

MOST POINTS IN A SEASON
100

CLUB RECORDS - GOALS

MOST GOALS SCORED IN A SEASON
106
Man. City (2017-18)

FEWEST GOALS CONCEDED IN A SEASON
15
Chelsea (2004-05)

MOST GOALS SCORED AT HOME IN A SEASON
68
Chelsea (2009-10)

MOST GOALS CONCEDED IN A SEASON
100
Swindon
(46-game season – 1993-94)

89
Derby
(38-game season – 2007-08)

BEST GOAL DIFFERENCE IN A SEASON
79
Man. City (2017-18)

WORST GOAL DIFFERENCE IN A SEASON
-69
Derby (2007-08)

FEWEST GOALS SCORED AT HOME IN A SEASON
10
Man. City (2006-07)

MOST GOALS CONCEDED AT HOME IN A SEASON
45
Swindon
(1993-94 – 21 games)

FEWEST GOALS SCORED IN A SEASON
20
Derby (2007-08)

CLUB RECORDS - POINTS

MOST POINTS IN A SEASON WHILE BEING RELEGATED

49
Crystal Palace
(46-game season – 1992-93)

42
West Ham United
(38-game season – 2002-03)

FEWEST POINTS IN A SEASON WHILE STAYING UP

34
West Brom (2004-05)

MOST POINTS IN A SEASON WITHOUT WINNING THE LEAGUE

89
Man. United (2011-12)

FEWEST HOME POINTS IN A SEASON

7
Sunderland (2005-06)

FEWEST AWAY POINTS IN A SEASON

3
Derby (2006-07)

FEWEST POINTS IN A SEASON WHILE WINNING THE LEAGUE

75
Man. United (1996-97)

MOST AWAY POINTS IN A SEASON

50
Man. City (2017-18)

CLUB RECORDS - WINS

MOST HOME WINS IN A SEASON (19 GAMES)
18
Chelsea (2005-06), Man. United (2010-11)
& Man. City (2011-12)

FEWEST HOME WINS IN A SEASON
1
Sunderland (2005-06)
& Derby (2007-08)

MOST CONSECUTIVE HOME WINS
20
Man. City
(5 March, 2011 to 21 March 2012)

MOST CONSECUTIVE AWAY WINS
11
Chelsea (6 April, 2008 to 7 December, 2008) &

Man. City (May 21, 2017 and December 27, 2017)

MOST DEFEATS IN A SEASON (42 OR 38 GAMES)
29
Ipswich (1994-95), Sunderland (2005-06)
& Derby (2007-08)

MOST CONSECUTIVE AWAY GAMES UNBEATEN
27
Arsenal
(April 5, 2003 to September 25, 2004)

ATTENDANCES

HIGHEST ATTENDANCE
83,222
Tottenham 1-0 Arsenal
(Wembley Stadium, February 10, 2018)

LOWEST ATTENDANCE
3,039
Wimbledon 1-3 Everton

(Selhurst Park, January 23, 1993)

PLAYER RECORDS

MOST PREMIER LEAGUE APPEARANCES
653
Gareth Barry
(May 2, 1998 to February 24, 2018)

MOST PREMIER LEAGUE SEASONS APPEARED IN
22
Ryan Giggs (every season from 1992-93 to 2013-14)

PLAYER RECORDS - GOALS

MOST PREMIER LEAGUE GOALS
260
Alan Shearer

MOST PREMIER LEAGUE GOALS AT ONE CLUB
183
Wayne Rooney (Man. United)

OLDEST GOALSCORER
40 years &
268 days
Teddy Sheringham (for West Ham v Portsmouth, December 26, 2006)

YOUNGEST GOALSCORER
16 years &
271 days
James Vaughan (for Everton v Crystal Palace, April 10, 2005)

MOST GOALS IN A PREMIERLEAGUE SEASON (38 GAMES)
32
Mohamed Salah
(2017-18)

MOST CONSECUTIVE PREMIER LEAGUE MATCHES SCORED IN
11
Jamie Vardy (August 29 to November 28, 2015)

MOST PREMIER LEAGUE SEASONS SCORED IN
21
Ryan Giggs (every season from 1992-93 to 2013-13)

MOST GOALS IN A PREMIER LEAGUE SEASON (42 GAMES)
34
Andrew Cole (1993-94) & Alan Shearer (1994-95)

MOST GAMES SCORED IN DURING A PREMIER LEAGUE SEASON
24
Mohamed Salah
(2017-18)

MOST CONSECUTIVE PREMIER LEAGUE APPEARANCES
310
Brad Friedel
(August 14, 2004 to October 7, 2012)

OLDEST PLAYER
John Burridge
43 years and 162 days
(for Man. City v QPR, May 14, 1995)

YOUNGEST PLAYER
Matthew Briggs Ⓥ
16 years and 65 days
(for Fulham v Middlesbrough, May 13, 2007)

FASTEST PREMIER LEAGUE HAT-TRICK
2 minutes 56 seconds
Sadio Mane
(Southampton v Aston Villa, May 16, 2015)

FASTEST GOAL
10 seconds
Ledley King
(for Tottenham v Bradford, December 9, 2000 at Valley Parade)

MOST OWN GOALS
10
Richard Dunne

MOST GOALS IN ONE HALF
5
Jermain Defoe
(for Tottenham v Wigan, November 22, 2009 at White Hart Lane)

MOST GOALS SCORED BY A SUBSTITUTE IN ONE GAME
4
Ole Gunnar Solskjaer
(for Man. United v Nottingham Forest, February 6, 1999 at the City Ground)

MOST GOALS IN A GAME 5

Andrew Cole (Man. United v Ipswich, March 4, 1995

Alan Shearer (Newcastle v Sheff. Wed., September 19, 1999)

Jermain Defoe (Tottenham v Wigan, November 22, 2009)

Dimitar Berbatov
(Man. United v Blackburn, November 27, 2010)

Sergio Aguero (Man. City Newcastle, October , 2015)

HIGH-SCORING GAMES

BIGGEST HOME WIN
9-0
Man. United v Ipswich
(March 4, 1995)

BIGGEST AWAY WIN
1-8
Nottingham Forest v Man.
United (February 9, 1999)

HIGHEST-SCORING GAME
7-4
Portsmouth v Reading
(September 29, 2007)

GOALKEEPER RECORDS

**MOST CLEAN SHEETS
IN A CAREER**
201
Petr Čech

**MOST CLEAN SHEETS
IN ONE SEASON**
24
Petr Čech
(for Chelsea, 2004-05)

**LONGEST RUN WITHOUT
CONCEDING A GOAL**
14 games
(1,311 minutes)
Edwin van der Sar
(for Man. United, 2008-09)

THE MANAGERS

MOST PREMIER LEAGUE TITLES
13
Sir Alex Ferguson
(1993, 1994, 1996, 1997, 1999, 2000, 2001,
2003, 2007, 2008, 2009, 2011, 2013)

MOST PROMOTIONS
TO THE PREMIER LEAGUE
4
Steve Bruce (Birmingham in 2001-02 &
2006-07 and Hull in 2012-13 & 2015-16)

MOST RELEGATIONS
FROM THE PREMIER LEAGUE
3
Dave Bassett (Sheff. United in 1993-94,
Nottingham Forest in 1996-97 & Leicester in 2001-02)

LONGEST SPELL AS MANAGER
21 years, 224 days
Arsene Wenger
(Arsenal, October 1,
1996 to May 13, 2018)

SHORTEST SPELL AS MANAGER
41 days (8 games)
Les Reed
(Charlton, November 14,
2006 to December 24, 2006)

DISCIPLINE

MOST RED CARDS
8
Duncan Ferguson,
Patrick Vieira &
Richard Dunne

MOST YELLOW CARDS
103
Gareth Barry

DREAM TEAM
THE PREMIER LEAGUE'S ALL TIME GREATEST TEAM

It might seem like an impossible task, trying to pick an all-time Premier League Dream Team. The Premier League has attracted many of the world's best players from all four corners of the globe, thanks to a combination of its reputation for being one of the most competitive leagues in the world, and the money clubs can use to entice them. So trying to choose the single best player for each position, over the 26 years the League has existed, would be the stuff of nightmares, wouldn't it? It would and it was, but regardless, it's been done. A team of 11 players at the top of their profession who have excelled week in, week out, not just for months, but consistently throughout their careers.

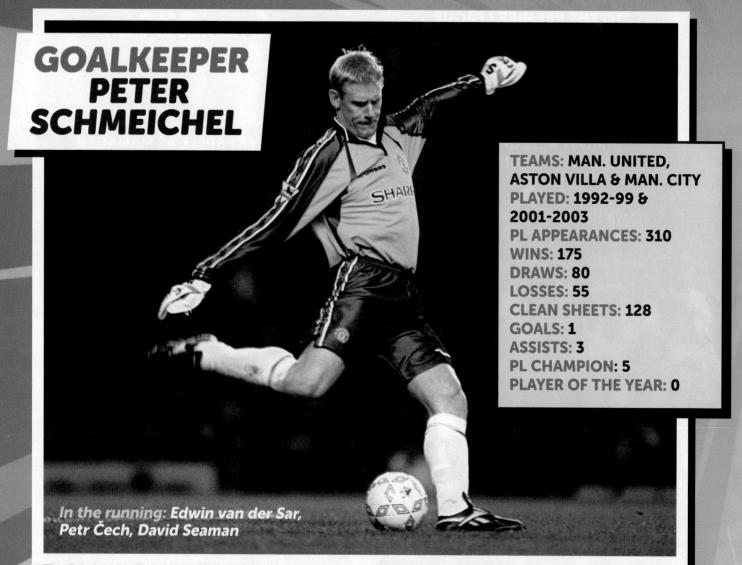

GOALKEEPER
PETER SCHMEICHEL

TEAMS: MAN. UNITED, ASTON VILLA & MAN. CITY
PLAYED: 1992-99 & 2001-2003
PL APPEARANCES: 310
WINS: 175
DRAWS: 80
LOSSES: 55
CLEAN SHEETS: 128
GOALS: 1
ASSISTS: 3
PL CHAMPION: 5
PLAYER OF THE YEAR: 0

In the running: Edwin van der Sar, Petr Čech, David Seaman

The Danish goalkeeper was already a European Championship winner when he arrived at United in 1991, and quickly established himself in the United side. Brave, imposing, commanding of his area and an incredible shot-stopper, the stopper won five Premier League titles in nine years at Old Trafford before moving to Sporting Lisbon. He returned to England for spells with Aston Villa, where he scored his only Premier League goal, before ending his career at Man. City.

RIGHT BACK
GARY NEVILLE

In the running: *Lee Dixon, Branislav Ivanovic, Lauren*

TEAMS: MAN. UNITED
PLAYED: 1992-2011
PL APPEARANCES: 400
WINS: 256
DRAWS: 87
LOSSES: 57
GOALS: 5
ASSISTS: 35
PL CHAMPION: X
PLAYER OF THE YEAR: 0

One-club Neville became United's first-choice right-back in 1994-95 after impressing in the United youth teams, and went on to make the right-back spot his own for the next 15 years. Tough, dependable, with great positioning and who rarely let his winger past him, Neville is one of United's most decorated players, winning eight Premier League titles in his total of 20 trophies while at the club. He was also appointed United's club captain after Roy Keane left, and made a total of 602 appearances for the Old Trafford club.

CENTRE BACK
RIO FERDINAND

In the running:
Sol Campbell,
Vincent Kompany,
Jaap Stam

TEAMS: WEST HAM, LEEDS, MAN. UNITED & QPR
PLAYED: 1995-2015
PL APPEARANCES: 504
WINS: 291
DRAWS: 110
LOSSES: 103
GOALS: 11
ASSISTS: 8
PL CHAMPION: 6
PLAYER OF THE YEAR: 0

Ferdinand broke the British transfer record when he signed for Man. United for £30 million in 2002, but quickly went about repaying Alex Ferguson's faith in him. On the ball the defender was calm, could bring the ball out of defence and had excellent distribution, but he also had great positional sense and timed his tackles to perfection. In 12 years at Old Trafford, Ferdinand won six Premier League titles, three League cups and a Champions League to establish himself as one of the best defenders in world football.

CENTRE BACK
JOHN TERRY

In the running:
Nemanja Vidic,
Tony Adams,
Ricardo Carvalho

TEAMS: CHELSEA
PLAYED: 1998-2017
PL APPEARANCES: 492
WINS: 311
DRAWS: 107
LOSSES: 74
GOALS: 41
ASSISTS: 12
PL CHAMPION: 5
PLAYER OF THE YEAR: 1

Terry came through Chelsea's ranks to become the most successful captain in their history, leading the Blues to five Premier League titles, five FA Cups, three League Cups, the Champions League and the Europa League. A strong, tenacious, commanding and physical defender, Terry excels in the air and is renowned for his tackling, positioning, ability to read the game and strong leadership. He left the club in 2017 after nearly 20 years at the Blues, and will go down as one of the finest defenders of his generation.

LEFT BACK
ASHLEY COLE

In the running:
Denis Irwin,
Patrice Evra,
Stuart Pearce

A defender who loved to attack, Ashley Cole was one of the best left-backs of his generation. He started his career at Arsenal, where he won two Premier League titles and three FA Cups an was an integral part of 'The Invincibles' side that went unbeaten during the 2003-04 Premier League campaign. Cole's pace made him a danger going forward, and his anticipation allowed him to cut out danger. In 2006 he moved to Chelsea, where he won the Premier League, Champions League and four more FA Cups, becoming the only player in history to win the FA Cup seven times.

TEAMS: ARSENAL & CHELSEA
PLAYED: 1999-2014
PL APPEARANCES: 385
WINS: 240
DRAWS: 88
LOSSES: 57
GOALS: 15
ASSISTS: 31
PL CHAMPION: 3
PLAYER OF THE YEAR: 0

RIGHT MIDFIELD
CRISTIANO RONALDO

TEAMS: MAN. UNITED
PLAYED: 2003-09
PL APPEARANCES: 196
WINS: 132
DRAWS: 36
LOSSES: 28
GOALS: 84
ASSISTS: 34
PL CHAMPION: 3
PLAYER OF THE SEASON: 2

In the running:
David Beckham,
Riyad Mahrez,
Steve McManaman

Cristiano Ronaldo arrived at Man. United in 2003 as a slight 18-year-old, and left six years later for a world record fee as arguably the best player on the planet. Blessed with lightning pace, quick feet, superb balance, a powerful shot and great ability in the air, Ronaldo scored 84 goals in 196 games, mainly from the right-wing. He won the Premier League title three times, scored in the 2008 Champions League final as United beat Chelsea on penalties and was also named the PFA Player Of The Year two years in a row. One of the finest players the Premier League has ever seen.

In the running:
Roy Keane,
Patrick Vieira,
Xabi Alonso

CENTRE MIDFIELD
STEVEN GERRARD

Liverpool-born Gerrard spent his entire Premier League career with the Reds and is surely the best player never to have lifted the trophy. After breaking into the first team in 1998 as an 18-year-old, he quickly established himself in the side and was made captain at the age of 23. The complete midfielder, Gerrard was able to play in both holding and attacking roles, as well as playing out wide and even at-full-back in his earlier days. A hard-working, box-to-box player, Gerrard was a ball-winner, tackled well, had a superb range of passing, read the game well and could score all kinds of goals, but especially from a distance.

TEAMS: **LIVERPOOL**
PLAYED: **1998-2015**
PL APPEARANCES: **504**
WINS: **255**
DRAWS: **130**
LOSSES: **119**
GOALS: **120**
ASSISTS: **92**
PL CHAMPION: **0**
PLAYER OF THE YEAR: **1**

119

In the running:
Frank Lampard,
Xabi Alonso,
David Silva

CENTRE MIDFIELD PAUL SCHOLES

TEAMS: MAN. UNITED
PLAYED: 1993-2011 &
2012-13
PL APPEARANCES: 499
WINS: 321
DRAWS: 106
LOSSES: 72
GOALS: 107
ASSISTS: 55
PL CHAMPION: 11
PLAYER OF THE SEASON: 0

Another member of Man. United's Class of '93 youth team, Scholes made his debut for the Red Devils in 1994 as a 19-year-old and quickly established himself in the team alongside captain Roy Keane. Blessed with incredible technical ability, great vision, awareness, a superb range of passing, ability to keep the ball under pressure and scoring from distance, Scholes became one of the best midfielders of his generation. The midfielder won ten Premier League titles before retiring in May 2011, only to be persuaded to return by Sir Alex Ferguson in January 2012, and won an 11th Premier League title in the 2012-13 season.

LEFT MIDFIELD RYAN GIGGS

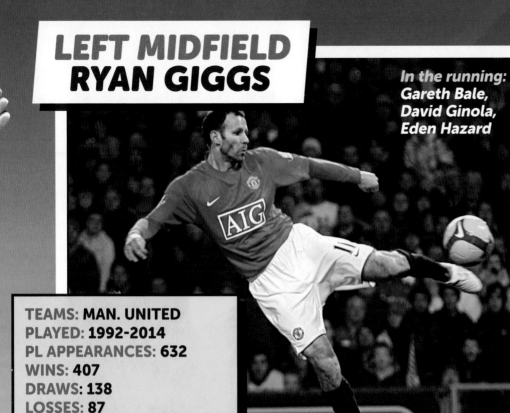

In the running: Gareth Bale, David Ginola, Eden Hazard

Premier League legends don't come any bigger than Ryan Giggs. The winger is the only player to have played in the first 22 seasons of the Premier League, and the only to have scored in the first 21. He made his debut in March 1991, 18 months before the Premier League started, and went on to make 963 appearances for the Red Devils, more than any United player. Giggs was blessed with electric speed, great control, superb balance, excellent crossing ability and a body swerve that allowed him to glide past defenders like they weren't there. He won 13 Premier League titles, four FA Cups, three League Cups and two Champions Leagues to become one of the most decorated players ever in British football.

TEAMS: MAN. UNITED
PLAYED: 1992-2014
PL APPEARANCES: 632
WINS: 407
DRAWS: 138
LOSSES: 87
GOALS: 109
ASSISTS: 162
PL CHAMPION: 13
PLAYER OF THE YEAR: 1

STRIKER ALAN SHEARER

In the running: Wayne Rooney, Sergio Aguero, Ruud van Nistelrooy

Shearer is the Premier League's all-time record scorer with 260 goals and scored 422 in all competitions, including internationals. If it hadn't been for a number of serious injuries in his career, the total would have been far higher. He started his career at Southampton, before moving to Blackburn for a British record of £3 million in 1992 prior to the first Premier League season. He won the title in 1995 before moving to Newcastle in 1996 for £15 million, again a British record at the time. Shearer was the typical British striker — strong, held the ball up well, was good in the air, had a fearsome shot, was lethal in the penalty area and only needed the mere sight of goal to score.

TEAMS: BLACKBURN & NEWCASTLE
PLAYED:
PL APPEARANCES: 441
WINS: 203
DRAWS: 109
LOSSES: 129
GOALS: 260
ASSISTS: 64
PL CHAMPION: 1
PLAYER OF THE YEAR: 2

STRIKER THIERRY HENRY

In the running:
Luis Suarez, Gianfranco Zola, Eric Cantona

TEAMS: ARSENAL
PLAYED: 1999-2007 & 2012
PL APPEARANCES: 258
WINS: 157
DRAWS: 62
LOSSES: 39
GOALS: 175
ASSISTS: 74
PL CHAMPION: 2
PLAYER OF THE SEASON: 2

When Henry joined Arsenal in 1999 he was primarily a winger, but under Arsene Wenger he became one of the most feared strikers in world football. In his two spells with the Gunners, Henry became the club's all-time leading scorer with 228 goals in all competitions, including 175 Premier League strikes. A lightning-quick forward who loved to run at defenders, he could score from distance or close range but he was particularly lethal in one-on-one situations, where his calmness and composure in front of goal meant he rarely missed. In his time at the club he won two Premier League titles, two FA Cups and was named PFA Player Of The Year on two occasions.

Peter
Schmeichel

Gary
Neville

Rio
Ferdinand

John
Terry

Ashley
Cole

Cristiano
Ronaldo

Paul
Scholes

Steven
Gerrard

Ryan
Giggs

Thierry
Henry

Alan
Shearer

THE BEST
PREMIER LEAGUE
QUOTES
EVER

"

Funny, philosophical, thought-provoking or just plain bonkers — football can make people say weird and wonderful things, so here are some of the best quotes the Premier League has to offer.

"

'Young players are like melons. Only when you open and taste the fruit are you 100 per cent sure that it's good. Sometimes you have beautiful melons but they don't taste good. Other times they're ugly but the taste is fantastic'

Jose Mourinho talks melons. As you do.

'I told him Newcastle was nearer to London than Middlesbrough, and he believed me.'

Newcastle United boss Kevin Keegan spun a few untruths to persuade Plaistow lad Robert Lee to leave Charlton and move north. It was a wise one — Lee spent ten years on Tyneside, racking up 379 games.

'When I score, I don't celebrate because it's my job. When a postman delivers letters, does he celebrate?'

Mario Balotelli on the art of celebrating a goal.

'My kids begged me not to sign them.'

West Ham Owner David Sullivan doesn't do himself any favours with two of his own players, Jose Fonte and Robert Snodgrass.

'In the past he was a little man in many circumstances, he is a little man in the present and for sure he will be a little man in the future.'

Antonio Conte was more than a little irritated by Jose Mourinho too.

'We must have had 99 per cent of the match. It was the other three per cent that cost us.'

Chelsea manager Ruud Gullit gets his maths slightly out after losing to Coventry in 1997. The Dutch legend replaced Glenn Hoddle in the summer of 1996, becoming player-manager.

'If you're a burglar, it's no good poncing about outside somebody's house, looking good with your swag bag ready. Just get in there, burgle them and come out. I don't advocate that obviously, it's just an analogy.'

Ian Holloway turned press conferences into spectacles with his unique grasp on the football lexicon.

'It is omelettes and eggs. No eggs — no omelettes! It depends on the quality of the eggs. In the supermarket you have class one, two or class three eggs and some are more expensive than others and some give you better omelettes. So when the class one eggs are in Waitrose and you cannot go there, you have a problem.'

Jose Mourinho using another food analogy when commenting on the lack of funds available to him to strengthen his Chelsea squad.

'We are breathing. We are not out of the hospital, but we are out of emergency and we can accept visits.'

Swansea manager Carlos Carvalhal after struggling Swansea's shock win over Liverpool.

'Sometimes you look in a field and see a cow. You think it's a better cow than the one you see in your field. It never really works out that way'

Manchester United manager Sir Alex Ferguson explaining why Wayne Rooney should stay at the club in 2010.

'I'm proud of it, the proudest man in Proudsville. I'm proud of it all.'

A proud Sean Dyche after Burnley climb proudly into the top four in the 2017-18 season.

'If you don't know the answer to that question, then I think you are an ostrich. Your head must be in the sand. Is your head in the sand? Are you flexible enough to get your head in the sand? My suspicion would be no.'

Leicester City manager Nigel Pearson's response when journalist Ian Baker asked him to clarify which criticism he had referred to in an earlier answer. Leicester had just lost 3-1 to Chelsea but their four consecutive wins beforehand and unbeaten finish afterwards secured their Premier League status. Just a few weeks after this meltdown, Pearson was out of a job.

'The only way to stop Thierry Henry? With a gun!'

Former Chelsea manager Gianluca Vialli might be on to something here as he talks about the damage Thierry Henry can cause if you're not careful.

'The trick is always buy when you're strong, so he needs to buy players. You can't win anything with kids. You look at that line up Manchester United had today and Aston Villa at quarter past two when they get the team sheet, it's just going to give them a lift and it will happen every time he plays the kids. He's got to buy players, as simple as that.'

Alan Hansen's infamous remarks on Match of the Day after Manchester United lost their first match of the 1995-96 season to Aston Villa. Following a summer overhaul of the squad, Alex Ferguson's line-up had a youthful complexion, with home-grown players Gary Neville, Phil Neville, Paul Scholes and Nicky Butt in the XI and David Beckham coming off the bench. It proved a minor set-back as the 'Fergie Fledglings' won the League and FA Cup double.

'I write like a two-year-old and I can't spell. I can't work a computer. I don't even know what an email is. I've never sent a fax or a text message. I'm the most disorganised person in the world. I can't even fill in the team-sheet.'

Harry Redknapp not presenting the best application for the England manager's job. He was speaking during a 2012 trial in which he was found not guilty of two counts of cheating the public revenue along with former Portsmouth chairman Milan Mandaric.

'It was time to put all the meat on the barbecue.'

Swansea manager Carlos Carvalhal after throwing all of his attackers off and being rewarded with a last-gasp win over Burnley.

'I'm out at the moment, but should you be the chairman of Barcelona, AC Milan or Real Madrid, I'll get straight back to you. The rest can wait.'

The answerphone message of Wimbledon manager Joe Kinnear during the 'Crazy Gang' days. Kinnear managed at Selhurst Park between January 1992 and June 1999, keeping the Dons in the top flight, sometimes miraculously.

'Do you think I would enter into a contract with that mob? Absolutely no chance. I would not sell them a virus. That is a 'No' by the way. There is no agreement whatsoever between the clubs.'

Sir Alex Ferguson when asked about rumours claiming Cristiano Ronaldo was set to join Real Madrid. It was December 2008 and Man. United, the reigning champions of Europe, were heading for another league title. Ronaldo duly moved to Madrid the following

'I tried to watch the Tottenham match on television in my hotel yesterday, but I fell asleep.'

Arsene Wenger with an absolute zinger at the expense of Arsenal's North London rivals.

'I think boring is ten years without a title – that's boring. If you support a club and you wait, wait, wait for so many years without a Premier League title, then that's boring.'

Jose Mourinho with one of his many digs at Arsenal and, more specifically, their manager Arsene Wenger, in 2015. While Chelsea cantered to the League title, Arsenal were desperate to end a drought

'I think he is one of these people who is a voyeur. He likes to watch other people. There are some guys who, when they are at home, have a big telescope to see what happens in other families. He speaks, speaks, speaks about Chelsea.'

Jose Mourinho's way of telling Arsenal manager Arsene Wenger to get his own house in order before speaking ill of his Chelsea team. It was October 2005 and Chelsea were some 14 points ahead of the Gunners in the Premier League table. Wenger had suggested Chelsea's belief would be affected by a 1-1 draw at Everton and a Carling Cup loss to Charlton. Chelsea would win the title by eight points and finished 24 ahead of Arsenal.

'But I want to talk about facts. I want to be clear, I do not want to play mind games too early, although they seem to want to start. But I have seen some facts...'

Rafa Benitez, boss of top-of-the-table Liverpool, gets paranoid about advantages afforded to Sir Alex Ferguson and his Manchester United side in January 2009. Pulling a piece of paper from his blazer pocket, Rafa proceeds to claim Ferguson receives preferential treatment from referees and preferential treatment from the fixture computer. But remember, these were not 'mind games', only 'facts.' United won the title by four points from Liverpool.

'When the seagulls follow the trawler, it is because they think sardines will be thrown into the sea.'

Eric Cantona had just escaped a two-week prison sentence for his kung-fu kick on Crystal Palace fan Matthew Simmons. Cantona uttered this immortal line, then stood up and walked out of the room, leaving the assembled media stunned. Eight months later, he would return from his suspension to help Manchester United to the Double.

'At the end of the day they need to get behind the team. Away from home our fans are fantastic, I'd call them the hardcore fans. But at home they have a few drinks and probably the prawn sandwiches, and they don't realise what's going on out on the pitch. I don't think some of the people who come to Old Trafford can spell football, never mind understand it. To win games by three and four every time - these people need fantasy football. They need to get in the real world.'

Manchester United captain Roy Keane's magnificent broadside at the prawn sandwich munchers in the Old Trafford hospitality boxes in 2000.

We have to carry on doing our best. It's getting tickly now - squeaky-bum time, I call it. It's going to be an interesting few weeks and the standard of the Premiership is such that nothing will be easy.'

Alex Ferguson describes the pressure of the title run-in back in 2003. 'Squeaky bum time' passed into common

'I could answer in many different ways but I am not going to lose my hair to speak about Antonio Conte.'

Jose Mourinho has a thinly-veiled dig at the Italian's hair.

'I'm very excited with this team because they are 'playerish' – if there is such a word – they love to play.'

Arsene Wenger offering a new addition to the Oxford English Dictionary as he waxed lyrical about his team during the 2007-08 season.

'Judging by the shape of his face, he must have headed a lot of goals.'

Former West Ham manager Harry Redknapp on Iain Dowie, who did indeed score plenty of goals during his playing days, though we're not sure how many were with his head.

'As we say in Portugal, they brought the bus and they left the bus in front of the goal.'

Jose Mourinho bemoans Tottenham's ultra-defensive style at Stamford Bridge to claim a draw.

'Please don't call me arrogant because what I am saying is true. I am European champion. I think I am the special one.'

Jose Mourinho announces his arrival to English football upon joining Chelsea as manager in 2004. He soon shook up the natural order of things, as the Blues dominated the Premier League for the following two seasons. An endless fascination with this born winner began.

'He could start a row in an empty house.'

Alex Ferguson has a clear view about Dennis Wise.

'When you do that with footballers like he said about Leeds, and when you do things like that about a man like Stuart Pearce. I've kept really quiet but I'll tell you something, he went down in my estimations when he said that. We have not resorted to that. You can tell him now, we're still fighting for this title and he's got to go to Middlesbrough and get something. And I'll tell you, honestly, I will love it if we beat them. Love it. But it really has got to me. I've voiced it live, not in front of the press or anywhere. I'm not even going to the press conference. But the battle is still on and Man United have not won this yet.'

Kevin Keegan's epic meltdown live on Sky Sports in 1996. Keegan's Newcastle team, who had sat 12 points clear of Man United in the title race at one stage, had seen their lead eroded and then their position usurped by Ferguson's unstoppable team.

SEASON
BY
SEASON

2017-18

Man. City swept aside the opposition to claim their third Premier League title and give manager Pep Guardiola his first domestic title in England.

City broke records all the way through the season, from being the first team to reach 100 points, to winning the League by 19 points and scoring a record 106 goals along the way. After finishing fourth the previous season, Guardiola spent over £160 million on new players including goalkeeper Ederson, Bernardo Silva, Kyle Walker, Benjamin Mendy and Danilo.

Their title rivals strengthened too, with Chelsea paying £60 million to sign Alvaro Morata. Arsenal and Man. United also signed new strikers, with Alexandre Lacazette arriving at the Emirates and Romelu Lukaku joining United from Everton for £75 million.

But it was Liverpool who would make the signing of the season, with Mohamed Salah arriving at Anfield from Roma for £34 million. The Egypt star set a new Premier League record for a 38-game season by scoring 32 goals on his

way to winning the PFA Player of the Year award.

For the first time, the Premier League season kicked off on a Friday night and it did so in dramatic fashion, with Arsenal coming from behind to beat Leicester 4-3 at The Emirates.

But the Gunners lost their next two games, away to Stoke 1-0 and 4-0 against Liverpool, which left them in 16th place at the end of August. It would be a sign of things to come, with Arsene Wenger's side only winning three games away from home all season, and none in 2018.

But if that was bad, Crystal Palace were even worse. The Eagles lost their first seven games without scoring before finally beating Champions Chelsea in October, but didn't win an away point or score an away goal until a 3-0 win at Leicester on December 16. Fortunately, the Eagles recovered from their shaky start to finish 11th.

It was Man. City who got off to the best start. After drawing with Everton 1-1 in their second game, City won every game to lead Man. United by 11 points by Christmas. In total, they won 18 games on the trot before eventually losing 4-3 at Liverpool on January.

They would only lose one more game that season. City could have claimed the title with a win over Man. United at the Etihad, but Jose Mourinho's side came away with a 3-2 win.

It meant City needed a favour from West Brom the following week to win the League. After City had defeated Tottenham 3-1, The Baggies beat Man. United 1-0 to hand City their third Premier League title.

Liverpool pipped Chelsea for the final Champions League place on the last day of the season, while at the other end of the table, West Brom, Stoke and Swansea were relegated to the Championship.

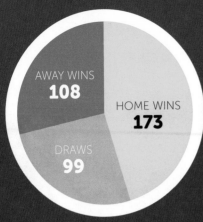

AWAY WINS
108

HOME WINS
173

DRAWS
99

GAMES PLAYED **380**

GOALS SCORED **1,018**

AVERAGE GOALS/GAME: **2.68**

TOP SCORERS

1. **Mohamed Salah** Liverpool — **32**
2. **Harry Kane** Tottenham — **30**
3. **Sergio Aguero** Man. City — **21**
4. **Jamie Vardy** Leicester City — **20**
5. **Raheem Sterling** Man. City — **18**
6. **Romelu Lukaku** Man. United — **16**
7. **Roberto Firmino** Liverpool — **15**

PFA PLAYER OF THE YEAR:
Mohamed Salah (Liverpool)

PFA YOUNG PLAYER OF THE YEAR:
Leroy Sane (Man. City)

GOAL OF THE SEASON:
Jamie Vardy, 10/03/18
West Brom v Leicester

STATS

Biggest transfer:
£75m Romelu Lukaku
(Everton to Man. United)

Biggest win:
Watford 0-6 Man. City

Longest winning run:
18 games (Man. City)

Longest winless run:
20 games (West Brom)

Longest losing run:
8 games (West Brom)

Highest attendance:
83,222 (Tottenham v Arsenal)

Lowest attendance:
10,242 (Bournemouth v West Brom)

Average attendance: 38,274

Longest unbeaten run:
22 games (Man. City)

TEAM OF THE SEASON

David de Gea

Kyle Walker · Nicolas Otamendi · Jan Vertonghen · Marcos Alonso

David Silva · Kevin De Bruyne · Christian Eriksen

Harry Kane · Sergio Aguero · Mohamed Salah

		P	W	D	L	F	A	GD	Pts
1	Man.City	38	32	4	2	106	27	79	100
2	Man.United	38	25	6	7	68	28	40	81
3	Tottenham	38	23	8	7	74	36	38	77
4	Liverpool	38	21	12	5	84	38	46	75
5	Chelsea	38	21	7	10	62	38	24	70
6	Arsenal	38	19	6	13	74	51	23	63
7	Burnley	38	14	12	12	36	39	-3	54
8	Everton	38	13	10	15	44	58	-14	49
9	Leicester	38	12	11	15	56	60	-4	47
10	Newcastle	38	12	8	18	39	47	-8	44
11	Crystal Palace	38	11	11	16	45	55	-10	44
12	Bournemouth	38	11	11	16	45	61	-16	44
13	West Ham	38	10	12	16	48	68	-20	42
14	Watford	38	11	8	19	44	64	-20	41
15	Brighton	38	9	13	16	34	54	-20	40
16	Huddersfield	38	9	10	19	28	58	-30	37
17	Southampton	38	7	15	16	37	56	-19	36
18	Swanse	38	8	9	21	28	56	-28	33
19	Stoke	38	7	12	19	35	68	-33	33
20	WBA	38	6	13	19	31	56	-25	31

2016-17

The 2016-17 season marked the Premier League's 25th anniversary, and it was Chelsea who regained the title after finishing the previous campaign in 10th place.

During a busy summer, the managerial merry-go-round saw eight appointments, with Italy coach Antonio Conte joining the Blues. There were also two new managers in Manchester, where old foes Jose Mourinho and Pep Gaurdiola renewed old rivalries at United and City respectively.

There were also a number of new signings, and none bigger than Paul Pogba's return to Man. United for a world record fee of £89 million just four years, after leaving the club to join Juventus.

Other notable arrivals were N'Golo Kante joining Chelsea from Leicester, Christian Benteke's £27 million move to Crystal Palace, Sadio Mane joining Liverpool, and Man. City signing Leroy Sane, Gabriel Jesus and John Stones.

It was City who got off to the best possible start with six successive Premier League wins, including a win at Old Trafford as Guardiola's men beat United 2-1.

After defeats to Liverpool and Arsenal, Chelsea looked anything but title contenders, but Antonio Conte changed their formation and it transformed their season, going on a run of 13 successive wins.

That run ended at Tottenham in January 2017, when the north Londoners showed their own title credentials as young England midfielder Dele Alli scored both goals in a 2-0 win.

Man. United went 25 games unbeaten between October and May, but 12 draws ended any title ambitions.

Leicester, who had won the League title so incredibly the season before, sacked manager Claudio Ranieri in February with the Foxes just above the relegation zone.

Assistant manager Craig Shakespeare took over and won his first five Premier League games in charge, the first a 3-1 win over Liverpool, and eventually led Leicester to 12th.

But the Reds went on to secure a top-four finish and a return to the Champions League, while Arsenal finished fifth and missed out for the first time in 20 years under Arsene Wenger.

Harry Kane's goals helped Tottenham win nine games on the trot between February and April to keep the pressure on Chelsea at the top of the table. However, a defeat at West Ham opened the door for the Blues to clinch the title at West Brom, and a 1-0 win handed Antonio Conte the Premier League title in his first season in England.

At the other end of the table there was disappointment for Hull, Middlesbrough and Sunderland, who were all relegated to the Championship.

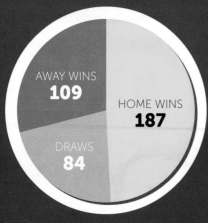

AWAY WINS **109**

HOME WINS **187**

DRAWS **84**

GAMES PLAYED **380**

GOALS SCORED **1,064**

AVERAGE GOALS/GAME: **2.80**

TOP SCORERS

1. **Harry Kane** Tottenham — **29**
2. **Romelu Lukaku** Everton — **25**
3. **Alexis Sanchez** Arsenal — **24**
4. **=Diego Costa** Chelsea — **20**
4. **=Sergio Aguero** Man. City — **20**
6. **Deli Alli** Tottenham — **18**
7. **Zlatan Imbrahimovic** Man. United — **17**

Longest unbeaten run: 25 games (Man. United)

STATS

Biggest transfer:
£90m Paul Pogba
(Juventus to Man. United)

Biggest win:
Hull 1-7 Tottenham

Longest winning run:
13 games (Chelsea)

Longest winless run:
16 games (Middlesbrough)

Longest losing run:
6 games (Crystal Palace, Hull & Watford)

Highest attendance:
75,397 (Man. United v West Brom)

Lowest Attendance:
10,890 (Bournemouth v Middlesbrough)

Average attendance:
35,821

David **de Gea**

Kyle **Walker** — Gary **Cahill** — David **Luiz** — Danny **Rose**

Eden **Hazard** — Deli **Alli** — N'Golo **Kante** — Sadio **Mane**

Harry **Kane** — Romelu **Lukaku**

TEAM OF THE SEASON

PFA PLAYER OF THE YEAR:
N'Golo Kante (Chelsea)

PFA YOUNG PLAYER OF THE YEAR:
Dele Alli (Tottenham)

GOAL OF THE SEASON:
Emre Can, 01/05/17
Watford v Liverpool

		P	W	D	L	F	A	GD	Pts
1	Chelsea	38	30	3	5	85	33	52	93
2	Tottenham	38	26	8	4	86	26	60	86
3	Man. City	38	23	9	6	80	39	41	78
4	Liverpool	38	22	10	6	78	42	36	76
5	Arsenal	38	23	6	9	77	44	33	75
6	Man.United	38	18	15	5	54	29	25	69
7	Everton	38	17	10	11	62	44	18	61
8	Southampton	38	12	10	16	41	48	-7	46
9	Bournemouth	38	12	10	16	55	67	-12	46
10	WBA	38	12	9	17	43	51	-8	45
11	West Ham	38	12	9	17	47	64	-17	45
12	Leicester	38	12	8	18	48	63	-15	44
13	Stoke	38	11	11	16	41	56	-15	44
14	Crystal Palace	38	12	5	21	50	63	-13	41
15	Swansea	38	12	5	21	45	70	-25	41
16	Burnley	38	11	7	20	39	55	-16	40
17	Watford	38	11	7	20	40	68	-28	40
18	Hull	38	9	7	22	37	80	-43	34
19	Middlesbrough	38	5	13	20	27	53	-26	28
20	Sunderland	38	6	6	26	29	69	-40	24

2015-16

The 2015-16 Premier League season will go down as one of the most incredible seasons in history. Leicester City, who only just escaped relegation in 2014-15 and were 5000/1 outsiders to win the League, somehow managed to do just that.

There were no signs in the close season that this would happen. The Foxes parted company with manager Nigel Pearson and replaced him with Claudio Ranieri, who had recently left his post as Greece manager after a nightmare spell in charge.

Champions Chelsea brought in Radamel Falcao and Pedro and despite losing Petr Čech to Arsenal, looked the team to beat. Man. City added Raheem Sterling and Kevin De Bruyne, while rivals United signed Anthony Martial from Monaco.

But while City got off to a great start, winning their first five matches, Chelsea were sitting just above the relegation zone at the end of September after suffering defeats to Man. City, Everton and Crystal Palace.

Manuel Pellegrini's side began to falter, and a 4-1 defeat to Tottenham put Spurs in contention for a top-four place. On the same day, Leicester's unbeaten start to the season ended when Arsenal won 5-2 at The King Power Stadium.

But Leicester recovered, not losing again until Boxing Day. Key to that was the form of Jamie Vardy, who set a new record of scoring in 11 successive matches to beat former Man. United striker Ruud van Nistelrooy's 10-match run in a 1-1 draw against United at the end of November.

A 2-1 win over Chelsea in early December saw the Foxes go top, while the Blues slipped down to 16th. That, as well as defeats to Southampton, Bournemouth and Liverpool, saw Jose Mourinho relieved of his duties.

Wins over Man. City and Man.

United took Arsenal top at the turn of the year. They had suffered a shock 4-0 defeat to Southampton on Boxing Day, but Leicester failed to capitalise, losing 2-1 at Liverpool on the same day.

But Ranieri's team rallied, winning at Tottenham before drawing 1-1 at Aston Villa, a result that took them top. The Foxes suffered a 2-1 stoppage-time defeat to Arsenal on February 14, which brought Arsene Wenger's men within two points of the leaders, but that was the last time Leicester would be defeated that season.

In fact, Ranieri's men went from strength to strength. Six wins without conceding a goal in the space of seven games, combined with Tottenham drawing against Liverpool and West Brom, left Leicester needing to beat Man. United to win their first top-flight title in their 132-year history.

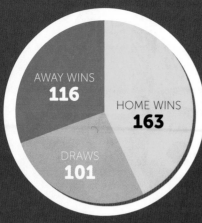

AWAY WINS **116**

HOME WINS **163**

DRAWS **101**

GAMES PLAYED **380**

GOALS SCORED **1,026**

AVERAGE GOALS/GAME: **2.70**

TOP SCORERS

1.	**Harry Kane** Tottenham	**26**	
2.	**=Sergio Aguero** Man. City	**24**	
2.	**=Jamie Vardy** Leicester	**24**	
4.	**Romelu Lukaku** Everton	**18**	
5.	**Riyad Mahrez** Leicester	**17**	
6.	**Olivier Giroud** Arsenal	**16**	
7.	**=2 Players**	**15**	

Longest winless run:
19 games (Aston Villa)

STATS

Biggest transfer:
£54.5m Kevin De Bruyne
(Wolfsburg to Man. City)

Biggest win:
Aston Villa 0-6 Liverpool

Longest winning run:
6 games (Tottenham)

Longest unbeaten run:
15 games (Chelsea)

Longest losing run:
11 games (Aston Villa)

Highest attendance:
75,415 (Man. United v Swansea)

Lowest attendance:
10,863 (Bournemouth v Stoke)

Average attendance:
36,451

David de Gea

Hector **Bellerin** | Toby **Alderweireld** | Wes **Morgan** | Danny **Rose**

Riyad **Mahrez** | Deli **Alli** | N'Golo **Kante** | Dimitri **Payet**

Harry **Kane** | Jamie **Vardy**

TEAM OF THE SEASON

PFA PLAYER OF THE YEAR:
Riyad Mahrez (Leicester)

PFA YOUNG PLAYER OF THE YEAR:
Dele Alli (Tottenham)

GOAL OF THE SEASON:
Dele Alli, 23/01/16
Crystal Palace v Tottenham

		P	W	D	L	F	A	GD	Pts
1	Leicester	38	23	12	3	68	36	32	81
2	Arsenal	38	20	11	7	65	36	29	71
3	Tottenham	38	19	13	6	69	35	34	70
4	Man. City	38	19	9	10	71	41	30	66
5	Man. United	38	19	9	10	49	35	14	66
6	Southampton	38	18	9	11	59	41	18	63
7	West Ham	38	16	14	8	65	51	14	62
8	Liverpool	38	16	12	10	63	50	13	60
9	Stoke City	38	14	9	15	41	55	-14	51
10	Chelsea	38	12	14	12	59	53	6	50
11	Everton	38	11	14	13	59	55	4	47
12	Swansea	38	12	11	15	42	52	-10	47
13	Watford	38	12	9	17	40	50	-10	45
14	WBA	38	10	13	15	34	48	-14	43
15	Crystal Palace	38	11	9	18	39	51	-12	42
16	Bournemouth	38	11	9	18	45	67	-22	42
17	Sunderland	38	9	12	17	48	62	-14	39
18	Newcastle	38	9	10	19	44	65	-21	37
19	Norwich	38	9	7	22	39	67	-28	34
20	Aston Villa	38	3	8	27	27	76	-49	17

2014-15

Jose Mourinho's Chelsea dominated the 2014-15 season, topping the table for a record 274 days to win the League by eight points and claim their fourth Premier League title.

The Blues, had been strengthened that summer with the signings of Cesc Fabregas from Barcelona and Atletico Madrid's Diego Costa, got off to a flying start. They won seven of their first eight games, including a 6-3 victory at Everton and a 2-0 triumph over Arsenal. The only points dropped in that run were at Man. City, where Blues legend Frank Lampard netted the equaliser in a 1-1 draw.

The traditional title challengers were finding life tough. Man. United were 3-1 up at newly-promoted Leicester only to lose 5-3, with Jamie Vardy playing a part in every goal for the Foxes. Liverpool, who had come so close to winning the Premier League the previous season, struggled to replicate

their form following Luis Suarez's departure to Barcelona.

But Chelsea faltered over Christmas and that allowed Man. City to move level on points, goal difference and goals scored on New Year's Day. The Blues then lost 5-3 to Tottenham on New Year's Day, with Harry Kane scoring twice.

Southampton, with Ronald Koeman in charge, were making a surprise bid for the top four. Despite losing key players the previous summer including Luke Shaw, Adam Lallana, Dejan Lovren, Rickie Lambert and Callum Chambers, the Saints moved up to third following wins over Arsenal, Man. United and Newcastle in January.

They eventually finished seventh, but with a club record 60 points, the second-best defence in the League and the fastest hat-trick in Premier League history – with Sadio Mane's treble against Aston Villa – illustrated a superb campaign.

The title race swung back in Chelsea's favour when Arsenal won 2-0 at Man. City, with the Blues moving four points clear. Tough games against Man. United and Liverpool were negotiated without any defeats, allowing them to claim the title at Crystal Palace in early May.

In the battle against relegation, Leicester, who were bottom at Christmas and looked dead and buried by the end of March, staged one of the Premier League's great escapes. The Foxes won seven of their last nine games to secure safety with a game to spare, eventually finishing 14th.

With QPR and Burnley already down, it meant it was a straight fight between Newcastle and Hull for survival. The Tigers gained an excellent draw against Man. United, but Newcastle's 2-0 win over West Ham condemned the East Yorkshire club to the Championship.

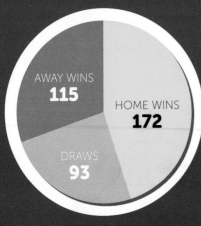

AWAY WINS
115

HOME WINS
172

DRAWS
93

GAMES
PLAYED **380**
GOALS
SCORED **975**

AVERAGE GOALS/GAME: **2.57**

TOP SCORERS

1. **Sergio Aguero** Man. City **26**

2. **Harry Kane** Tottenham **21**

3. **Diego Costa** Chelsea **20**

4. **Charlie Austin** QPR **18**

5. **Alexis Sanchez** Arsenal **16**

6. **=3 players** **14**

PFA PLAYER OF THE YEAR:
Eden Hazard (Chelsea)

PFA YOUNG PLAYER OF THE YEAR:
Harry Kane (Tottenham)

GOAL OF THE SEASON:
Jack Wilshere, 24/05/15
Arsenal v West Brom

STATS

Biggest transfer:
£60m Angel Di Maria
(Real Madrid to Man. United)

Biggest win:
Southampton 8-0 Sundelrand

Longest winning run:
8 games (Arsenal)

Longest unbeaten run:
16 games (Chelsea)

Longest losing run:
8 games (Newcastle)

Highest attendance:
75,454 (Man. United v West Brom)

Lowest attendance:
16,163 (QPR v Stoke)

Average attendance: 36,175

Longest winless run:
13 games (Leicester)

TEAM OF THE SEASON

Team of the Season lineup:
- David de Gea
- Branislav Ivanovic, John Terry, Gary Cahill, Ryan Bertrand
- Alexis Sanchez, Nemanja Matic, Philippe Coutinho, Eden Hazard
- Harry Kane, Diego Costa

		P	W	D	L	F	A	GD	Pts
1	Chelsea (C)	38	26	9	3	73	32	41	87
2	Man. City	38	24	7	7	83	38	45	79
3	Arsenal	38	22	9	7	71	36	35	75
4	Man. United	38	20	10	8	62	37	25	70
5	Tottenham	38	19	7	12	58	53	5	64
6	Liverpool	38	18	8	12	52	48	4	62
7	Southampton	38	18	6	14	54	33	21	60
8	Swansea	38	16	8	14	46	49	-3	56
9	Stoke	38	15	9	14	48	45	3	54
10	Crystal Palace	38	13	9	16	47	51	-4	48
11	Everton	38	12	11	15	48	50	-2	47
12	West Ham	38	12	11	15	44	47	-3	47
13	WBA	38	11	11	16	38	51	-13	44
14	Leicester	38	11	8	19	46	55	-9	41
15	Newcastle	38	10	9	19	40	63	-23	39
16	Sunderland	38	7	17	14	31	53	-22	38
17	Aston Villa	38	10	8	20	31	57	-26	38
18	Hull	38	8	11	19	33	51	-18	35
19	Burnley	38	7	12	19	28	53	-25	33
20	QPR	38	8	6	24	42	73	-31	30

2013-14

Man. United entered a new era without Sir Alex Ferguson, the most successful manager in British history and one who had dominated the Premier League since its inception.

Former Everton boss David Moyes was his successor, but he struggled with the enormity of the role and it allowed Manchester rivals City, who themselves had a new manager in Manuel Pellegrini, to claim their second Premier League crown.

The Manchester clubs weren't the only ones with new managers. Roberto Martinez left Wigan to replace David Moyes at Everton, while Jose Mourinho returned to Chelsea for a second spell after leaving Real Madrid.

However, the early season pacesetters were managed by one of the League's longest-serving managers. Arsenal, under Arsene Wenger, recovered from

an opening-day defeat to win 11 of their first 13 matches. A 6-3 defeat at Man. City saw them briefly knocked off top spot, but they quickly regrouped and were top going into 2014.

They finally relinquished top spot in February following a 5-1 thrashing at the hands of Liverpool. That was the first of 11 consecutive wins for the Reds, including a 3-0 win over Man. United at Old Trafford and a dramatic 3-2 win over Man. City at Anfield.

Liverpool were five points clear at the top with just three games to go, and looked set to end a 24-year wait for a top-flight title. However, Chelsea travelled to Anfield and won 2-0, in a game where Steven Gerrard's slip allowed Demba Ba a free run on goal to make it 2-0 and seal the win.

Things got worse in the next game at Crystal Palace when, after

leading 3-0 with just 12 minutes left, the Reds conceded three times as Palace salvaged a 3-3 draw.

Man. City took advantage, winning 4-0 at home to Aston Villa before beating West Ham on the last day of the season. City had only spent 15 days at the top of the table all season, but it was enough to claim their second Premier League title.

Elsewhere, Everton and Tottenham secured Europa League football after edging out Man. United, who finished outside the top three for the first time in Premier League history.

At the bottom, Sunderland became only the second side to recover from being bottom at Christmas to avoid the drop. Instead, Cardiff's first season in the Premier League ended with an instant return to the Championship, and they were joined by Norwich and Fulham.

Season stats

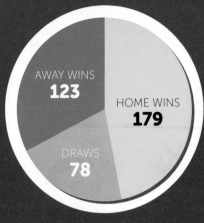

AWAY WINS **123**

HOME WINS **179**

DRAWS **78**

GAMES PLAYED **380**

GOALS SCORED **1,052**

AVERAGE GOALS/GAME: **2.77**

TOP SCORERS

1.	**Luis Suarez** Liverpool	**31**
2.	**Daniel Sturridge** Liverpool	**21**
3.	**Yaya Toure** Man. City	**20**
4.	**=Wayne Rooney** Man. United	**17**
4.	**=Wilfred Bony** Swansea	**17**
4.	**=Sergio Aguero** Man. City	**17**
7.	**=2 Players**	**16**

Longest losing run:
7 games (Crystal Palace)

STATS

Biggest transfer:
£42.5m Mesut Ozil
(Real Madrid to Arsenal)

Biggest win:
Man. City 7-0 Norwich

Longest winning run:
11 games (Liverpool)

Longest unbeaten run:
16 games (Liverpool)

Longest winless run:
9 games (Fulham, Sunderland & West Brom)

Highest attendance:
75,368 (Man. United v Aston Villa)

Lowest Attendance:
19,242 (Swansea v Stoke)

Average attendance:
36,657

TEAM OF THE SEASON

Petr **Cech**

Seamus **Coleman**
Gary **Cahill**
Vincent **Kompany**
Luke **Shaw**

Adam **Lallana**
Steven **Gerrard**
Yaya **Toure**
Edan **Hazard**

Luis **Suarez**
Daniel **Sturridge**

PFA PLAYER OF THE YEAR:
Luis Suarez (Liverpool)

PFA YOUNG PLAYER OF THE YEAR:
Eden Hazard (Chelsea)

GOAL OF THE SEASON:
Jack Wilshere, 19/10/13 Arsenal v Norwich

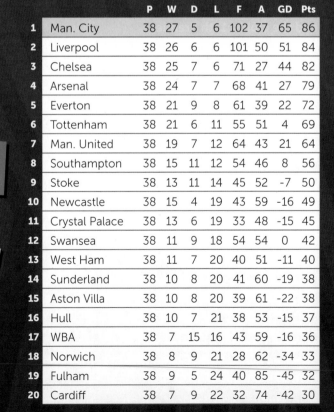

		P	W	D	L	F	A	GD	Pts
1	Man. City	38	27	5	6	102	37	65	86
2	Liverpool	38	26	6	6	101	50	51	84
3	Chelsea	38	25	7	6	71	27	44	82
4	Arsenal	38	24	7	7	68	41	27	79
5	Everton	38	21	9	8	61	39	22	72
6	Tottenham	38	21	6	11	55	51	4	69
7	Man. United	38	19	7	12	64	43	21	64
8	Southampton	38	15	11	12	54	46	8	56
9	Stoke	38	13	11	14	45	52	-7	50
10	Newcastle	38	15	4	19	43	59	-16	49
11	Crystal Palace	38	13	6	19	33	48	-15	45
12	Swansea	38	11	9	18	54	54	0	42
13	West Ham	38	11	7	20	40	51	-11	40
14	Sunderland	38	10	8	20	41	60	-19	38
15	Aston Villa	38	10	8	20	39	61	-22	38
16	Hull	38	10	7	21	38	53	-15	37
17	WBA	38	7	15	16	43	59	-16	36
18	Norwich	38	8	9	21	28	62	-34	33
19	Fulham	38	9	5	24	40	85	-45	32
20	Cardiff	38	7	9	22	32	74	-42	30

2012-13

Sir Alex Ferguson signed off his final season in charge of Manchester United with his, and the club's, 13th Premier League title.

The Scot ended his 27-year tenure at the club in style, winning the League by an impressive 13-point margin.

The summer of 2012 saw significant changes. One-club legends Paul Scholes and Jamie Carragher retired following incredible careers at Man. United and Liverpool respectively, while Premier League legends Michael Owen and Phil Neville also called time on their careers.

There were a number of new faces, too. Brendan Rodgers took over at Liverpool, with Denmark legend Michael Laudrup replacing him at Swansea, while Steve Clarke was named manager of West Brom.

Man. United, who had lost out on

the title the previous season in such dramatic fashion, signed Robin van Persie and Shinji Kagawa, while Arsenal snapped up Olivier Giroud to replace him as well as midfielder Santi Cazorla. Chelsea signed Eden Hazard from Lille for £32 million, Christian Benteke joined Aston Villa and Swansea snapped up Michu for £2 million, which would prove to be shrewd business.

Chelsea topped the table going into November but failed to win during the whole of the month and manager Roberto Di Matteo, who had won the Champions League with the Blues just six months earlier, was replaced with Rafael Benitez.

They were replaced by Man. United, who went through December unbeaten and opened up a seven-point advantage over their nearest rivals, Man. City.

That lead had stretched to 12 points by February after Man. City lost to

newly-promoted Southampton, while United showed no signs of faltering until they lost to their city rivals at Old Trafford thanks to a goal from Sergio Aguero.

The title was sealed when Robin van Persie, who won the Golden Boot in his first season at Old Trafford, scored a hat-trick in a 3-0 win over Aston Villa in April, including an incredible volley from outside the area.

Sir Alex Ferguson's final game in charge of Man. United was remarkable. United travelled to The Hawthorns to take on West Brom, and on-loan striker Romelu Lukaku scored a second-half hat-trick to salvage a 5-5 draw with the champions.

Man. City finished as runners-up, with Chelsea in third and Arsenal filling the fourth Champions League spot after winning 26 points from their final ten games.

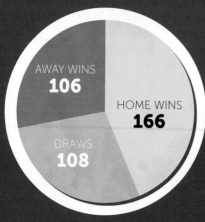

AWAY WINS
106

HOME WINS
166

DRAWS
108

GAMES PLAYED **380**
GOALS SCORED **1,063**
AVERAGE GOALS/GAME: **2.80**

TOP SCORERS

1. **Robin van Persie** — Man. United **26**
2. **Luis Suarez** — Liverpool **23**
3. **Gareth Bale** — Tottenham **21**
4. **Christian Benteke** — Aston Villa **19**
5. **Michu** — Swansea **18**
6. **Romelu Lukaku** — WBA **17**
7. **=4 Players** **15**

Longest winless run:
16 games (QPR)

STATS

Biggest transfer:
£32m Eden Hazard
(Lille to Chelsea)

Biggest win:
Chelsea 8-0 Aston Villa

Longest winning run:
7 games (Man. United)

Longest unbeaten run:
18 games (Man. United)

Longest losing run:
7 games (Reading)

Highest attendance:
75,605 (Man. United v Reading)

Lowest attendance:
15,436 (Wigan v Reading)

Average attendance:
35,931

David **de Gea**

Pablo **Zabaleta** — Rio **Ferdinand** — Jan **Vertonghen** — Leighton **Baines**

Edan **Hazard** — Michael **Carrick** — Juan **Mata** — Gareth **Bale**

Luis **Suarez** — Robin **van Persie**

TEAM OF THE SEASON

PFA PLAYER OF THE YEAR:
Gareth Bale (Tottenham)

PFA YOUNG PLAYER OF THE YEAR:
Gareth Bale (Tottenham)

GOAL OF THE SEASON:
Robin van Persie, 22/04/13
Man. United v Aston Villa

		P	W	D	L	F	A	GD	Pts
1	Man. United	38	29	4	5	86	43	43	91
2	Man. City	38	23	9	6	66	34	32	78
3	Chelsea	38	22	9	7	75	39	36	75
4	Arsenal	38	21	10	7	72	37	35	73
5	Tottenham	38	21	9	8	66	46	20	72
6	Everton	38	16	15	7	55	40	15	63
7	Liverpool	38	16	13	9	71	43	28	61
8	WBA	38	14	7	17	53	57	-4	49
9	Swansea	38	11	13	14	47	51	-4	46
10	West Ham	38	12	10	16	45	53	-8	46
11	Norwich	38	10	14	14	41	58	-17	44
12	Fulham	38	11	10	17	50	60	-10	43
13	Stoke	38	9	15	14	34	45	-11	42
14	Southampton	38	9	14	15	49	60	-11	41
15	Aston Villa	38	10	11	17	47	69	-22	41
16	Newcastle	38	11	8	19	45	68	-23	41
17	Sunderland	38	9	12	17	41	54	-13	39
18	Wigan	38	9	9	20	47	73	-26	36
19	Reading	38	6	10	22	43	73	-30	28
20	QPR	38	4	13	21	30	60	-30	25

2011-12

Man. City claimed their first Premier League crown, and their first top-flight title in 44 years, in the most dramatic fashion possible. Roberto Mancini's men scored two stoppage-time goals to win the League on goal difference from Man. United and send the Etihad into near bedlam.

Both City and rivals Man. United were neck-and-neck after winning their first four games, and that set the tone for the rest of the season. In August, Edin Dzeko scored four times as City hammered Tottenham 5-1 at White Hart Lane, before a Wayne Rooney hat-trick helped United smash Arsenal 8-2 at Old Trafford.

It was City who took early charge of the title race, dropping just four points from their first 14 games. This included a stunning 6-1 win against United at Old Trafford, with Mario Balotelli scoring twice and grabbing the headlines by revealing a 'Why Always Me?' t-shirt in celebration.

Tottenham were the Manchester clubs' nearest rivals at the turn of

the year but a 3-2 win for City at the Etihad effectively ended their title hopes.

United went on an eight-game winning run to go eight points clear at the top, but two defeats, including a 1-0 loss at City, left their rivals ahead in goal difference going into the final day.

City just needed to beat QPR to be crowned champions for the first time. But after Pablo Zabaleta had given them the lead, goals from Djibril Cisse and Jamie Mackie gave the Londoners a surprise 2-1 lead.

This, coupled with Man. United's 1-0 win at Sunderland, put United on the brink of their 13th Premier League title. But with QPR down to ten men after Joey Barton's dismissal, City came back. Edin Dzeko levelled the score in the 92nd minute and then, with

virtually the last kick of the match, Balotelli set up Aguero to smash the ball home to claim the title.

Newcastle secured Europa League football thanks to a run of seven wins from their final eight games of the season, with new signing Papiss Cisse scoring 13 goals in 14 matches after joining the Magpies.

At the other end of the table, Wigan staged a remarkable recovery to secure their Premier League survival. The Latics were bottom of the table in March, but a run of seven wins from their last nine, matches, including wins over Man. United, Arsenal, Newcastle and Liverpool, saw them finish the season in 15th.

That left Wolves, Blackburn and Bolton in the bottom three and consigned them to Championship football the following season.

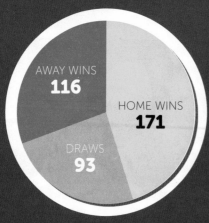

AWAY WINS
116

HOME WINS
171

DRAWS
93

GAMES PLAYED **380**

GOALS SCORED **1,066**

AVERAGE GOALS/GAME: **2.81**

TOP SCORERS

1. **Robin van Persie** **30**
   Arsenal

2. **Wayne Rooney** **27**
   Man. United

3. **Sergio Aguero** **23**
   Man. City

4. **=Clint Dempsey** **17**
   Fulham

4. **=Emmanual Adebayor** **17**
   Tottenham

4. **=Yakubu** **17**
   Blackburn

7. **Demba Ba** **16**
   Newcastle

PFA PLAYER OF THE YEAR:
Robin van Persie (Arsenal)

PFA YOUNG PLAYER OF THE YEAR:
Kyle Walker (Tottenham)

GOAL OF THE SEASON:
Papiss Cisse, 02/05/12
Chelsea v Newcastle

STATS

Biggest transfer:
£38m Sergio Aguero
(Atletico Madrid to Man. City)

Biggest win:
Man. United 8-2 Arsenal

Longest winning run:
8 games (Man. United)

Longest winless run:
12 games (Wolves)

Longest losing run:
8 games (Wigan)

Highest attendance:
75,627 (Man. United v Wolves)

Lowest attendance:
15,195 (QPR v Bolton)

Average attendance: 34,601

Longest unbeaten run:
14 games (Man. City)

TEAM OF THE SEASON

Joe **Hart**

Kyle **Walker** · Vincent **Kompany** · Fabricio **Coloccini** · Leighton **Baines**

David **Silva** · Yaya **Toure** · Scott **Parker** · Gareth **Bale**

Robin **van Persie** · Wayne **Rooney**

		P	W	D	L	F	A	GD	Pts
1	Man. City	38	28	5	5	93	29	64	89
2	Man. United	38	28	5	5	89	33	56	89
3	Arsenal	38	21	7	10	74	49	25	70
4	Tottenham	38	20	9	9	66	41	25	69
5	Newcastle	38	19	8	11	56	51	5	65
6	Chelsea	38	18	10	10	65	46	19	64
7	Everton	38	15	11	12	50	40	10	56
8	Liverpool	38	14	10	14	47	40	7	52
9	Fulham	38	14	10	14	48	51	-3	52
10	WBA	38	13	8	17	45	52	-7	47
11	Swansea	38	12	11	15	44	51	-7	47
12	Norwich	38	12	11	15	52	66	-14	47
13	Sunderland	38	11	12	15	45	46	-1	45
14	Stoke	38	11	12	15	36	53	-17	45
15	Wigan	38	11	10	17	42	62	-20	43
16	Aston Villa	38	7	17	14	37	53	-16	38
17	QPR	38	10	7	21	43	66	-23	37
18	Bolton	38	10	6	22	46	77	-31	36
19	Blackburn	38	8	7	23	48	78	-30	31
20	Wolves	38	5	10	23	40	82	-42	25

2010-11

Man. United won their 12th Premier League crown and 19th top-flight title, beating second-placed Chelsea by nine points.

The Blues went into the season as defending champions and started where they left off, winning their first five games, including back-to-back 6-0 wins over West Brom and Wigan.

Man. City made a number of big signings in Roberto Mancini's first full season in charge, including the arrivals of Yaya Touré from Barcelona and Spain international David Villa from Valencia.

Man. United beat Newcastle 3-0 on the opening weekend, with Ryan Giggs scoring for the 19th consecutive Premier League season. A 3-2 win over Liverpool soon followed, who had former Fulham boss Roy Hodgson in charge.

Liverpool briefly slipped into the bottom three following four defeats from their opening eight games, a run of form that saw Hodgson lose his job. That included a defeat by Premier League newcomers Blackpool, who found themselves in eighth place at the turn of the year.

In the January transfer window, Liverpool sold striker Fernando Torres to Chelsea for a British record £50 million fee and replaced him with Luis Suarez from Ajax and Newcastle's Andy Carroll.

Man. United topped the table going into the new year, having gone the first half of the season unbeaten. However, that record came to an end when they were defeated 2-1 by Wolves in their 26th game.

Arsenal were close behind in second, but one of the matches of the season would see the start of a series of dropped points for the Gunners. They travelled to Newcastle in February and cruised into a 4-0 lead, but after going down to ten men the Magpies came back and snatched an incredible 4-4 draw thanks to a long-range strike from Chieck Tiote.

A week later, Wayne Rooney's brilliant overhead kick helped United win the Manchester derby 2-1, a result which took the Red Devils four points clear at the top. United stayed in top spot for the rest of the season, and went six points clear of Chelsea with two games left after beating the Blues at Old Trafford, effectively securing the title.

At the other end of the table, Wolves came back from 3-0 down on the final day to lose 3-2 to Blackburn, but those two goals were enough to keep them up on goal difference, with Birmingham relegated instead. The Blues joined West Ham and Blackpool, who made an instant return to the Championship.

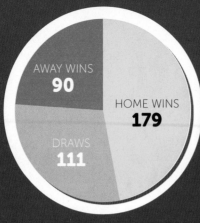

AWAY WINS
90

HOME WINS
179

DRAWS
111

GAMES PLAYED **380**

GOALS SCORED **1,063**

AVERAGE GOALS/GAME: **2.80**

TOP SCORERS

1. **Dimitar Berbatov**
Tottenham — **20**

2. **Carlos tevez**
Man. City — **20**

3. **Robin van Persie**
Arsenal — **18**

4. **Darren Bent**
Sunderland/Aston Villa — **17**

5. **Peter Odemwingie**
WBA — **15**

6. **=6 Players** — **13**

Longest winless run:
10 games (Blackburn)

STATS

Biggest transfer:
£50m Fernando Torres,
(Liverpool to Chelsea)

Biggest win:
Man. United 7-1 Blackburn

Longest winning run:
5 games (Chelsea)

Longest unbeaten run:
24 games (Man. United)

Longest losing run:
5 games (Blackpool, Bolton,
(West Brom & West Ham)

Highest attendance:
75,486 (Man. United v Bolton)

Lowest attendance:
14,042 (Wigan v Wolves)

Average attendance:
35,190

Edwin **van der Sar**

Bacary **Sagna** Nemanja **Vidic** Vincent **Kompany** Ashley **Cole**

Nani Samir **Nasri** Jack **Wilsher** Gareth **Bale**

Carlos **Tevez** Dimitar **Berbatov**

TEAM OF THE SEASON

PFA PLAYER OF THE YEAR:
Gareth Bale (Tottenham)

PFA YOUNG PLAYER OF THE YEAR:
Jack Wilshere (Arsenal)

GOAL OF THE SEASON:
Wayner Rooney, 12/02/11
Man. United v Man. City

		P	W	D	L	F	A	GD	Pts
1	Man. United	38	23	11	4	78	37	41	80
2	Chelsea	38	21	8	9	69	33	36	71
3	Man. City	38	21	8	9	60	33	27	71
4	Arsenal	38	19	11	8	72	43	29	68
5	Tottenham	38	16	14	8	55	46	9	62
6	Liverpool	38	17	7	14	59	44	15	58
7	Everton	38	13	15	10	51	45	6	54
8	Fulham	38	11	16	11	49	43	6	49
9	Aston Villa	38	12	12	14	48	59	-11	48
10	Sunderland	38	12	11	15	45	56	-11	47
11	WBA	38	12	11	15	56	71	-15	47
12	Newcastle	38	11	13	14	56	57	-1	46
13	Stoke	38	13	7	18	46	48	-2	46
14	Bolton	38	12	10	16	52	56	-4	46
15	Blackburn	38	11	10	17	46	59	-13	43
16	Wigan	38	9	15	14	40	61	-21	42
17	Wolves	38	11	7	20	46	66	-20	40
18	Birmingham	38	8	15	15	37	58	-21	39
19	Blackpool	38	10	9	19	55	78	-23	39
20	West Ham	38	7	12	19	43	70	-27	33

THE 00's

2009-10

Man. United's quest for an unprecedented fourth consecutive title was thwarted by Chelsea, who claimed their third Premier League crown under new manager Carlo Ancelotti.

Much had changed since their title win the previous May. Cristiano Ronaldo had joined Real Madrid for a world-record fee while talismanic striker Carlos Tevez crossed Manchester to join rivals City.

United were strengthened by the capture of Antonio Valencia from Wigan and Michael Owen from Newcastle. But the Red Devils didn't get off to a great start, losing to newly-promoted Burnley 1-0 at Turf Moor thanks to a Robbie Blake thunderbolt.

The early pace was set by Chelsea, who won their opening six games to sit at the top of the table, while Man. City and Spurs both started with four consecutive wins. But

when City travelled to Old Trafford to take on United on September 20, a stoppage-time strike by Michael Owen condemned them to a 4-3 defeat.

A run of seven consecutive draws saw City slip out of the title race, and in December it cost Mark Hughes his job. He was replaced by Roberto Mancini, who was given the task of closing the gap on Chelsea, Spurs and Aston Villa.

Chelsea topped the table at the turn of the year but Arsenal, inspired by Cesc Fabregas, briefly took over top spot in March following a run of six consecutive wins. However, the Gunners' title charge tailed off as they drew away at newly-promoted Birmingham before winning only seven more points from their final six games.

Chelsea regained the top spot at the start of April after beating Man. United 2-1 at Old Trafford, and then

won three of their next four games to hold a one-point advantage over United going into the last day of the season.

The Blues sealed the title in style, smashing eight goals past Wigan at Stamford Bridge to give Carlo Ancelotti his first Premier League title, and Chelsea's third in total. Their total of 103 goals in the Premier League was a new record, and they became the first top-flight team to hit a century of goals since Spurs in 1962-63.

At the other end of the table, Portsmouth, who had gone into administration and were deducted nine points, finished bottom. Hull finished one placed above them following struggles that had continued from the end of the previous campaign, while Burnley made an instant return to the Championship.

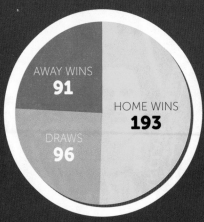

AWAY WINS **91**

HOME WINS **193**

DRAWS **96**

GAMES PLAYED **380**

GOALS SCORED **1,053**

AVERAGE GOALS/GAME: **2.77**

TOP SCORERS

1. **Didier Drogba** — Chelsea — **29**
2. **Wayne Rooney** — Man. United — **26**
3. **Darren Bent** — Sunderland — **24**
4. **Carlos tevez** — Man. City — **23**
5. **Frank Lampard** — Middlesbrough — **22**
6. =**Fernando Torres** — Liverpool — **18**
6. =**Jermain Defoe** — Tottenham — **18**

PFA PLAYER OF THE YEAR:
Wayne Rooney (Man. United)

PFA YOUNG PLAYER OF THE YEAR:
James Milner (Aston Villa)

GOAL OF THE SEASON:
Maynor Figueroa, 12/12/09
Stoke v Wigan

STATS

Biggest transfer:
£24.65m Carlos Tevez
(Man. United to Man. City)

Biggest win:
Tottenham 9-1 Wigan

Longest unbeaten run:
12 games (Birmingham)

Longest winless run:
14 games (Sunderland)

Longest losing run:
7 games (Portsmouth)

Highest attendance:
75,316 (Man. United v Stoke)

Lowest attendance:
14,323 (Wigan v Portsmouth)

Average attendance: 34,150

Longest winning run:
6 games (Arsenal & Chelsea)

TEAM OF THE SEASON

Joe **Hart**

Branislav **Ivanovic** — Thomas **Vermaelan** — Richard **Dunne** — Patrice **Evra**

Antonio **Valencia** — Cesc **Fabregas** — Darren **Fletcher** — James **Milner**

Wayne **Rooney** — Didier **Drogba**

		P	W	D	L	F	A	GD	Pts
1	Chelsea	38	27	5	6	103	32	71	86
2	Man. United	38	27	4	7	86	28	58	85
3	Arsenal	38	23	6	9	83	41	42	75
4	Tottenham	38	21	7	10	67	41	26	70
5	Man. City	38	18	13	7	73	45	28	67
6	Aston Villa	38	17	13	8	52	39	13	64
7	Liverpool	38	18	9	11	61	35	26	63
8	Everton	38	16	13	9	60	49	11	61
9	Birmingham	38	13	11	14	38	47	-9	50
10	Blackburn	38	13	11	14	41	55	-14	50
11	Stoke	38	11	14	13	34	48	-14	47
12	Fulham	38	12	10	16	39	46	-7	46
13	Sunderland	38	11	11	16	48	56	-8	44
14	Bolton	38	10	9	19	42	67	-25	39
15	Wolves	38	9	11	18	32	56	-24	38
16	Wigan	38	9	9	20	37	79	-42	36
17	West Ham	38	8	11	19	47	66	-19	35
18	Burnley	38	8	6	24	42	82	-40	30
19	Hull	38	6	12	20	34	75	-41	30
20	Portsmouth	38	7	7	24	34	66	-32	19

2008-09

But across Manchester a new era was just beginning. The Abu Dhabi United Group agreed a takeover of City, and after appointing Mark Hughes as their manager, made a number of new additions, including Vicent Kompany, Pablo Zabaleta and Robinho, who arrived from Real Madrid for a club record transfer fee.

Chelsea, under new manager Luiz Felipe Scolari, got off to a great start, picking up 20 points from their first eight matches. They were level on points with Liverpool, and surprise package Hull, by the end of October.

The newly-promoted Tigers won six of their first nine matches in their first Premier League season, including away wins at Arsenal and Tottenham. Spurs' defeat to Hull left the North Londoners at the bottom of the League, and led to manager Juande Ramos being replaced by Harry Redknapp.

Man. United were eight points behind leaders Chelsea and Liverpool after 12 games but a 5-0 thrashing of Stoke started a 16-match unbeaten run that helped them go top of the table in January.

Chelsea had fallen away but Liverpool, thanks to inspirational skipper Steven Gerrard and striker Fernando Torres, were firmly in the title race. Indeed, a 2-0 win over Chelsea and a 3-2 win at Portsmouth briefly put the Reds top in February, and a 4-1 win at Man. United signalled their intentions.

United were reeling, but the Red Devils swung the title race back in their favour when 17-year-old debutant Federico Macheda scored a late winner against Aston Villa to put Alex Ferguson's men one point ahead with a game in hand.

Liverpool's title hopes suffered a further blow when Andriy Arshavin scored all four goals in Arsenal's 4-4 draw with Liverpool at Anfield. United only dropped two more points in the remainder of the campaign and claimed their third consecutive title win with a game to spare.

The battle to beat the drop was fascinating. Hull, who had won only twice since their brilliant start to the season, were one point ahead of 18th-placed Newcastle, who now had legend Alan Shearer in charge.

The Tigers were beaten 1-0 at home to Man. United but Newcastle couldn't capitalise, losing 1-0 at Aston Villa to end their 16-year stay in the Premier League and condemn them to the Championship with West Brom and Middlesbrough.

TOP SCORERS

1. **Nicolas Anelka** 19
   Chelsea

2. **Cristiano Ronaldo** 18
   Man. United

3. **Steven Gerrard** 16
   Liverpool

4. **=Robinho** 14
   Man. City

4. **=Fernando Torress** 14
   Liverpool

5. **=5 Players** 12

Longest unbeaten run:
21 games (Arsenal)

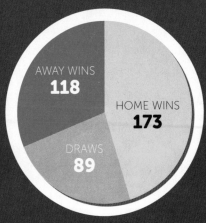

AWAY WINS **118**

HOME WINS **173**

DRAWS **89**

GAMES PLAYED 380

GOALS SCORED 942

AVERAGE GOALS/GAME: **2.48**

STATS

Biggest transfer:
£32.5m Robinho
(Real Madrid to Man. City)

Biggest win:
Man. City 6-0 Portsmouth

Longest winning run:
11 games (Man. United)

Longest winless run:
14 games (Middlesbrough)

Longest losing run:
6 games (Blackburn & Hull)

Highest attendance:
75,569 (Man. United v Liverpool)

Lowest attendance:
14,169 (Wigan v West Ham)

Average attendance:
35,650

TEAM OF THE SEASON

Edwin **van der Sar**

Glen **Johnson**

Nemanja **Vidic**

Rio **Ferdinand**

Patrice **Evra**

Cristiano **Ronaldo**

Steven **Gerrard**

Ashley **Young**

Ryan **Giggs**

Nicolas **Anelka**

Fernando **Torres**

PFA PLAYER OF THE YEAR:
Ryan Giggs (Man. United)

PFA YOUNG PLAYER OF THE YEAR:
Ashley Young (Aston Villa)

GOAL OF THE SEASON:
Glenn Johnson, 22/11/08
Portsmouth v Hull

		P	W	D	L	F	A	GD	Pts
1	Man. United	38	28	6	4	68	24	44	90
2	Liverpool	38	25	11	2	77	27	50	86
3	Chelsea	38	25	8	5	68	24	44	83
4	Arsenal	38	20	12	6	68	37	31	72
5	Everton	38	17	12	9	55	37	18	63
6	Aston Villa	38	17	11	10	54	48	6	62
7	Fulham	38	14	11	13	39	34	5	53
8	Tottenham	38	14	9	15	45	45	0	51
9	West Ham	38	14	9	15	42	45	-3	51
10	Man. City	38	15	5	18	58	50	8	50
11	Wigan	38	12	9	17	34	45	-11	45
12	Stoke	38	12	9	17	38	55	-17	45
13	Bolton	38	11	8	19	41	53	-12	41
14	Portsmouth	38	10	11	17	38	57	-19	41
15	Blackburn	38	10	11	17	40	60	-20	41
16	Sunderland	38	9	9	20	34	54	-20	36
17	Hull	38	8	11	19	39	64	-25	35
18	Newcastle	38	7	13	18	40	59	-19	34
19	Middlesbrough	38	7	11	20	28	57	-29	32
20	WBA	38	8	8	22	36	67	-31	32

BARCLAYS PREMIER LEAGUE
CHAMP10NS
2008

UEFA CHAMPIONS LEAGUE
WINN3RS
2008

2007-08

Man. United claimed their tenth Premier League title in just 15 years with forward Cristiano Ronaldo hitting 31 goals in the process, a joint-record for a 38-game season.

The Red Devils, who were defending their crown, strengthened in the summer, signing Owen Hargreaves, Nani, Anderson and Carlos Tevez. Liverpool signed Fernando Torres from Atletico Madrid while Arsenal, who saw all-time top scorer Thierry Henry leave, signed Croatia striker Eduardo.

Despite Henry's move to Spain, Arsenal enjoyed a great start, winning eight of their first nine matches. Key to that was striker Emmanual Adebayor, who scored the Goal Of The Season at in a 3-1 win in September.

But things weren't going so smoothly at Chelsea, and Jose Mourinho left the club after picking up 11 points from their first six

matches. He was replaced by Avram Grant, and the new manager suffered a 2-0 defeat to Man. United in his first game in charge.

At the turn of the year, Arsenal topped the table following one defeat in their first 21 matches. Man. United were close behind, with top scorer Cristiano Ronaldo in scintillating form. The Portugal forward scored an amazing, dipping free-kick against Portsmouth in a 2-0 win at the end of January that put The Red Devils top on goal difference.

Arsenal regained top spot when United lost to Man. City 3-0 in February, on an emotional day that marked the 50-year anniversary of the Munich Air Disaster. But following a 2-2 draw at Birmingham, the Gunners only won one of their next eight matches to seriously dent their title ambitions.

Chelsea, meanwhile, had played themselves back into contention. Following their defeat at United the

Blues had only lost once more, so when they won the reverse fixture on April 26 with a Michael Ballack double, they started to believe. However, United won their last two games to claim the title for a tenth time.

On the same day Chelsea beat United, Fulham began one of the greatest escapes in Premier League history. The Cottagers were five points from safety with three games left, and 2-0 down at Man. City with 20 minutes remaining.

But somehow they came back to win 3-2 and, after beating Birmingham in their following game, secured their safety with a 1-0 win against Portsmouth on the final day. Reading went down on goal difference despite a 4-0 win over already relegated Derby, who finished the season on a record-low 11 points for the season. They were joined by Birmingham, who were relegated despite a 4-1 win over Blackburn on the final day.

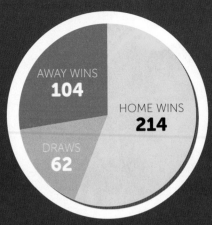

AWAY WINS
104

HOME WINS
214

DRAWS
62

GAMES PLAYED 380
GOALS SCORED 1,002

AVERAGE GOALS/GAME: **2.64**

TOP SCORERS

1. **Cristiano Ronaldo** Man. United — **31**
2. **=Fernando Torres** Blackburn — **24**
2. **=Emmanuel Adebayor** Arsenal — **24**
4. **Roque Santa Cruz** Blackburn — **19**
5. **=Benjani** Portsmouth/Man. City — **15**
5. **=Dimitar Berbatov** Tottenham — **15**
5. **=Robbie Keane** Tottenham — **15**

Longest unbeaten run:
21 games (Chelsea)

STATS

Biggest transfer:
£20m Fernando Torres
(Atletico Madrid to Liverpool)

Biggest win:
Middlesbrough 8-1 Man. City

Longest winning run:
8 games (Man. United)

Longest winless run:
32 games (Derby)

Longest losing run:
8 games (Reading & Wigan)

Highest attendance:
76,013 (Man. United v West Ham)

Lowest attendance:
14,007 (Wigan v Middlesbrough)

Average attendance:
36,076

David **James**

Bacary **Sagna** — Nemanja **Vidic** — Rio **Ferdinand** — Gael **Clichy**

Cristiano **Ronaldo** — Steven **Gerrard** — Cesc **Fabregas** — Ashley **Young**

Emmanuel **Adebayor** — Fernando **Torres**

TEAM OF THE SEASON

PFA PLAYER OF THE YEAR:
Cristiano Ronaldo (Man. United)

PFA YOUNG PLAYER OF THE YEAR:
Cesc Fabregas (Arsenal)

GOAL OF THE SEASON:
Emmanuel Adebayor, 15/09/07
Tottenham v Arsenal

		P	W	D	L	F	A	GD	Pts
1	Man. United	38	27	6	5	80	22	58	87
2	Chelsea	38	25	10	3	65	26	39	85
3	Arsenal	38	24	11	3	74	31	43	83
4	Liverpool	38	21	13	4	67	28	39	76
5	Everton	38	19	8	11	55	33	22	65
6	Aston Villa	38	16	12	10	71	51	20	60
7	Blackburn	38	15	13	10	50	48	2	58
8	Portsmouth	38	16	9	13	48	40	8	57
9	Man. City	38	15	10	13	45	53	-8	55
10	West Ham	38	13	10	15	42	50	-8	49
11	Tottenham	38	11	13	14	66	61	5	46
12	Newcastle	38	11	10	17	45	65	-20	43
13	Middlesbrough	38	10	12	16	43	53	-10	42
14	Wigan	38	10	10	18	34	51	-17	40
15	Sunderland	38	11	6	21	36	59	-23	39
16	Bolton	38	9	10	19	36	54	-18	37
17	Fulham	38	8	12	18	38	60	-22	36
18	Reading	38	10	6	22	41	66	-25	36
19	Birmingham	38	8	11	19	46	62	-16	35
20	Derby	38	1	8	29	20	89	-69	11

2006-07

Man. United denied Chelsea a hat-trick of consecutives Premier League titles, with Alex Ferguson's side securing their ninth in the process.

It was a crown the Blues didn't give up without a fight. During the summer, Jose Mourinho strengthened his squad with the signings of AC Milan striker Andriy Shevchenko, Germany international Michael Ballack from Bayern Munich and Arsenal defender Ashley Cole.

Elsewhere, West Ham made a statement by signing Carlos Tevez and Javier Mascherano, two of Argentina's stars from the World Cup that summer, while Man. United snapped up midfielder Michael Carrick from Tottenham for £16 million.

It was a move that paid dividends straight away, with the Red Devils setting the early pace. They hit four goals in 15 minutes in their first game against Fulham, which

ended in a 5-1 win, and went on to claim victories in their opening four games.

Bolton mounted an early challenge for the top four after an impressive start, but were beaten by leaders Man. United at the end of October, with Wayne Rooney scoring a hat-trick in a 4-0 win.

United, with Sir Alex Ferguson celebrating 20 years in charge, were relentless in their charge for the title and opened up a nine-point gap on their nearest rivals after winning all their games in February.

In April, Chelsea closed the gap on the Red Devils after a run of nine successive wins, but United were still five points ahead going into the final three games of the season. The Blues' next match was against Arsenal at the Emirates,

and following a 1-1 draw, United were crowned champions with two games to spare.

The battle to beat the drop was an exciting affair. West Ham, who were ten points adrift of safety at the start of March, won seven of their last nine games to beat the drop. Carlos Tevez scored for the Hammers on the final day at champions Man. United to claim a 1-0 win and ensure their safety.

That meant either Sheffield United or Wigan would join Watford and Charlton, and the two sides met on the final day at Bramall Lane. With the score at 1-1 in the second half, Wigan won a penalty. David Unsworth, who had only moved from United to Wigan in January, stepped up to take it and scored, sending his former club down in the process.

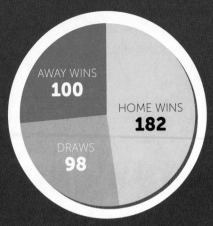

- AWAY WINS **100**
- HOME WINS **182**
- DRAWS **98**

GAMES PLAYED **380**
GOALS SCORED **931**

AVERAGE GOALS/GAME: **2.45**

TOP SCORERS

1. **Didier Drogba** — Chelsea — **20**
2. **Benni McCarthy** — Blackburn — **18**
3. **Cristiano Ronaldo** — Man. United — **17**
4. =**Wayne Rooney** — Man. United — **14**
4. =**Mark Viduka** — Middlesbrough — **14**
6. =**Darren Bent** — Charlton — **13**
6. =**Kevin Doyle** — Reading — **13**

PFA PLAYER OF THE YEAR:
Cristiano Ronaldo (Man. United)

PFA YOUNG PLAYER OF THE YEAR:
Cristiano Ronaldo (Man. United)

GOAL OF THE SEASON:
Wayne Rooney, 17/03/07
Man. United v Bolton

STATS

Biggest transfer:
£30m Andriy Shevchenko
(AC Milan to Chelsea)

Biggest win:
Reading 6-0 West Ham

Longest winning run:
9 games (Chelsea)

Longest unbeaten run:
14 games (Chelsea)

Longest losing run:
8 games (Wigan)

Highest attendance:
76,098 (Man. United v Blackburn)

Lowest attendance:
13,760 (Watford v Blackburn)

Average attendance: 34,402

Longest winless run:
11 games (Aston Villa, Watford & West Ham)

TEAM OF THE SEASON

Edwin **van der Sar**

Gary **Nevile** — Nemanja **Vidic** — Rio **Ferdinand** — Patrice **Evra**

Cristiano **Ronaldo** — Steven **Gerrard** — Paul **Scholes** — Ryan **Giggs**

Dimitar **Berbatov** — Didier **Drogba**

		P	W	D	L	F	A	GD	Pts
1	Man. United	38	28	5	5	83	27	56	89
2	Chelsea	38	24	11	3	64	24	40	83
3	Liverpool	38	20	8	10	57	27	30	68
4	Arsenal	38	19	11	8	63	35	28	68
5	Tottenham	38	17	9	12	57	54	3	60
6	Everton	38	15	13	10	52	36	16	58
7	Bolton	38	16	8	14	47	52	-5	56
8	Reading	38	16	7	15	52	47	5	55
9	Portsmouth	38	14	12	12	45	42	3	54
10	Blackburn	38	15	7	16	52	54	-2	52
11	Aston Villa	38	11	17	10	43	41	2	50
12	Middlesbrough	38	12	10	16	44	49	-5	46
13	Newcastle	38	11	10	17	38	47	-9	43
14	Man. City	38	11	9	18	29	44	-15	42
15	West Ham	38	12	5	21	35	59	-24	41
16	Fulham	38	8	15	15	38	60	-22	39
17	Wigan	38	10	8	20	37	59	-22	38
18	Sheff. United	38	10	8	20	32	55	-23	38
19	Charlton	38	8	10	20	34	60	-26	34
20	Watford	38	5	13	20	29	59	-30	28

2005-06

Jose Mourinho's Midas touch continued as he guided Chelsea to back-to-back Premier League titles. The Blues dominated the League once again, finishing eight points ahead of second-placed Arsenal.

But they didn't always have things their own way, never more so than on the opening day of the season, when they travelled to newly-promoted Wigan. The Latics pushed the title winners all the way, and it needed an injury-time winner from Hernan Crespo to see The Blues win 2-1.

Man. United, who were in an unfamiliar position of looking for their first title win in three seasons, inflicted Chelsea's first defeat of the season when they won 1-0 at Old Trafford in November.

England striker Michael Owen returned to England following a spell at Real Madrid and joined Newcastle, where he joined up with his old international strike partner, Alan Shearer. Owen scored a hat-trick against West Ham in December, but suffered from injuries and managed seven goals from just 11 games that season.

Shearer became the club's all-time top scorer in a 2-0 win over Portsmouth in February, and hit his 260th and final Premier League goal when he scored from the penalty spot in a 4-1 win over rivals Sunderland at the Stadium Of Light in April.

At the turn of the year Chelsea were 11 points clear at the top, with Man. United and Liverpool their nearest rivals. With the Blues holding such a commanding advantage, Man. United responded by signing defenders Nemanja Vidić and Patrice Evra.

It galvanised the Red Devils, who closed the gap on Chelsea to seven points, but a surprise draw at home to Sunderland in April took Chelsea to the brink of the title.

That title was secured against Man. United at the end of the month. William Gallas, Ricardo Carvalho and a brilliant Joe Cole strike saw the Blues win 3-0 and claim the trophy with two games to spare.

The battle for fourth place went to the final day, where Tottenham held a one-point advantage over Arsenal going into the final day. But they lost 2-1 to West Ham and Arsenal, who played their last game at Highbury before moving to their new stadium, beat Wigan 4-2. Thierry Henry hit a hat-trick, securing him the Golden Boot.

At the other end of the table, Portsmouth were eight points adrift of safety in March, but a run of six wins from their last nine matches secured their safety. That meant Birmingham, West Brom and Sunderland all suffered relegation to the Championship.

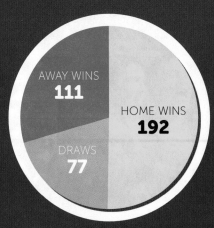

AWAY WINS **111**

HOME WINS **192**

DRAWS **77**

GAMES PLAYED **380**

GOALS SCORED **944**

AVERAGE GOALS/GAME: **2.48**

TOP SCORERS

1. **Thierry Henry** — Arsenal — **27**
2. **Ruud van Nistelrooy** — Man. United — **21**
3. **Darren Bent** — Charlton — **18**
4. =**Robbie Keane** — Tottenham — **16**
4. =**Frank Lampard** — Chelsea — **16**
4. =**Wayne Rooney** — Man. United — **16**
7. =**Marlon Harewood** — West Ham — **14**

Longest winning run:
10 (Chelsea & Liverpool)

STATS

Biggest transfer:
£24.4m Michael Essien
(Lyon to Chelsea)

Biggest win:
Arsenal 7-0 Middlesbrough

Longest unbeaten run:
13 games (Chelsea)

Longest winless run:
14 games (Sunderland)

Longest losing run:
9 games (Sunderland)

Highest attendance:
73,006 (Man. United v Charlton)

Lowest attendance:
16,550 (Fulham v Birmingham)

Average attendance:
33,875

Shay **Given**

Pascal **Chimbonda** · John **Terry** · William **Gallas** · Jamie **Carragher**

Cristiano **Ronaldo** · Steven **Gerrard** · Frank **Lampard** · Joe **Cole**

Thierry **Henry** · Wayne **Rooney**

TEAM OF THE **SEASON**

PFA PLAYER OF THE YEAR:
Steven Gerrard (Liverpool)

PFA YOUNG PLAYER OF THE YEAR:
Wayne Rooney (Man. United)

GOAL OF THE SEASON:
Steven Gerrard, 13/05/06
Liverpool v West Ham (FA Cup)

		P	W	D	L	F	A	GD	Pts
1	Chelsea	38	29	4	5	72	22	50	91
2	Man. United	38	25	8	5	72	34	38	83
3	Liverpool	38	25	7	6	57	25	32	82
4	Arsenal	38	20	7	11	68	31	37	67
5	Tottenham	38	18	11	9	53	38	15	65
6	Blackburn	38	19	6	13	51	42	9	63
7	Newcastle	38	17	7	14	47	42	5	58
8	Bolton	38	15	11	12	49	41	8	56
9	West Ham	38	16	7	15	52	55	-3	55
10	Wigan	38	15	6	17	45	52	-7	51
11	Everton	38	14	8	16	34	49	-15	50
12	Fulham	38	14	6	18	48	58	-10	48
13	Charlton	38	13	8	17	41	55	-14	47
14	Middlesbrough	38	12	9	17	48	58	-10	45
15	Man. City	38	13	4	21	43	48	-5	43
16	Aston Villa	38	10	12	16	42	55	-13	42
17	Portsmouth	38	10	8	20	37	62	-25	38
18	Birmingham	38	8	10	20	28	50	-22	34
19	WBA	38	7	9	22	31	58	-27	30
20	Sunderland	38	3	6	29	26	69	-43	15

2004-05

Chelsea celebrated their first ever Premier League title triumph, and their first top-flight title win for 50 years.

It was down in no small part to Jose Mourinho, the coach who had replaced Claudio Ranieri that summer after leading unfashionable Porto to Champions League glory.

Mourinho was supported with a huge transfer kitty by billionaire owner Roman Abramovich that saw Petr Čech, Ricardo Carvalho, Didier Drogba and Eidur Gudjohnsen arrive at Stamford Bridge.

And it was Gudjohnsen who got the Blues off to the perfect start, beating Man. United at Old Trafford on the opening weekend of the season.

United's response was to sign 18 year old Wayne Rooney from Everton for £27 million after impressing for England at Euro 2004, and the young striker went on to score 11 goals in his first season at Old Trafford.

Arsenal continued where their Invincible season had left off, breaking Nottingham Forest's 42-game record with a 5-3 win at home to Middlesbrough. The Gunners won eight of their first nine Premier League games, but their unbeaten record ended with a 2-0 defeat to Man. United on October 24, having gone 49 games without defeat.

Chelsea were Arsenal's nearest rivals, and soon after a defeat to Man. City, moved into top spot in November with a 1-0 win over Everton. It would prove to be Chelsea's only defeat of the season.

The Blues went from strength to strength, enjoying a five-point lead at the top of the table at Christmas and extending that to 11 points by February following an eight-match winning run.

The Blues were dominant, and broke Premier League records galore on their way to the title. The team won the most games, conceded fewest goals and kept the most clean sheets on their way to claiming their first Premier League title.

At the other end of the table, the final day of the season proved to be a dramatic one. Newly promoted Norwich, Crystal Palace and West Brom were battling with Southampton to avoid the drop. Norwich lost 6-0 at Fulham to be relegated, while Southampton's 2-1 defeat against Man. United meant they were down, too.

A late Charlton leveller meant that Palace were the team to join them, while West Brom became the first Premier League team to avoid relegation after being bottom of the table at Christmas.

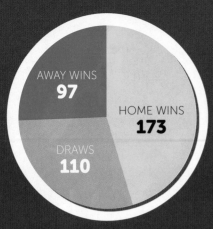

AWAY WINS
97

HOME WINS
173

DRAWS
110

GAMES PLAYED **380**

GOALS SCORED **975**

AVERAGE GOALS/GAME: **2.57**

TOP SCORERS

1. **Thierry Henry** Arsenal **25**

2. **Andy Johnson** Crystal Palace **21**

3. **Robert Pires** Arsenal **14**

4. **=Jermain Defoe** Tottenham **13**

4. **=Jimmy Flod Hasselbaink** Middlesbrough **13**

4. **=Frank Lampard** Chelsea **13**

4. **=Yakubu** Everton **13**

Longest winless run:
15 games (West Brom)

STATS

Biggest transfer:
£24m Didier Drogba
(Marseille to Chelsea)

Biggest win:
Arsenal 7-0 Everton

Longest winning run:
8 games (Chelsea)

Longest unbeaten run:
29 games (Chelsea)

Longest losing run:
6 games (Bolton & Tottenham)

Highest attendance:
67,989 (Man. United v Portsmouth)

Lowest attendance:
16,180 (Fulham v West Brom)

Average attendance:
33,893

Petr **Cech**

Gary **Neville** · John **Terry** · Rio **Ferdinand** · Ashley **Cole**

Shaun **Wright-Phillips** · Steven **Gerrard** · Frank **Lampard** · Arjen **Robben**

Thierry **Henry** · Andrew **Johnson**

TEAM OF THE **SEASON**

PFA PLAYER OF THE YEAR:
John Terry (Chelsea)

PFA YOUNG PLAYER OF THE YEAR:
Wayne Rooney (Man. United)

GOAL OF THE SEASON:
Wayne Rooney, 29/01/05
Man. United v Middlesbrough

		P	W	D	L	F	A	GD	Pts
1	Chelsea	38	29	8	1	72	15	57	95
2	Arsenal	38	25	8	5	87	36	51	83
3	Man. United	38	22	11	5	58	26	32	77
4	Everton	38	18	7	13	45	46	-1	61
5	Liverpool	38	17	7	14	52	41	11	58
6	Bolton	38	16	10	12	49	44	5	58
7	Middlesbrough	38	14	13	11	53	46	7	55
8	Man. City	38	13	13	12	47	39	8	52
9	Tottenham	38	14	10	14	47	41	6	52
10	Aston Villa	38	12	11	15	45	52	-7	47
11	Charlton	38	12	10	16	42	58	-16	46
12	Birmingham	38	11	12	15	40	46	-6	45
13	Fulham	38	12	8	18	52	60	-8	44
14	Newcastle	38	10	14	14	47	57	-10	44
15	Blackburn	38	9	15	14	32	43	-11	42
16	Portsmouth	38	10	9	19	43	59	-16	39
17	WBA	38	6	16	16	36	61	-25	34
18	Crystal Palace	38	7	12	19	41	62	-21	33
19	Norwich	38	7	12	19	42	77	-35	33
20	Southampton	38	6	14	18	45	66	-21	32

2003-04

The 2003-04 season went down in history as Arsenal went through the entire season unbeaten, winning the Premier League by 11 points and earning the title of 'The Invincibles'.

Arsène Wenger's side won 26 and drew 12 of their 38 Premier League games, and became the first side since Preston North End way back in 1889 to go through a season without suffering a single defeat.

Few would have predicted this at the start of the season. Chelsea had been bought by Russian billionaire Roman Abramovich and signed superstars like Hernan Crespo and Claude Makelele as manager Claudio Ranieri sought to bring the title to Stamford Bridge.

Man. United signed promising Portuguese winger Cristiano Ronaldo from Sporting Lisbon, and the impact he would have on the Premier League was beyond anyone's comprehension.

He took the No.7 shirt, which had been freed up by David Beckham's move to Real Madrid, and the 18-year-old had an instant impact, playing a part in three goals in Man. United's opening day 4-0 win over Bolton.

United team-mate Ruud van Nistelrooy was also making headlines, setting a new Premier League record by scoring in ten consecutive games. Strikes against Bolton and Newcastle at the start of the season took his tally to ten, with the other eight coming at the tail-end of the previous season.

Arsenal also started strongly, and topped the League when they faced Man. United in September for the first time that season. The game ended 0-0, but was remembered for a controversial penalty awarded to Man. United, only for Van Nistelrooy to miss.

Early on in the season, a number of surprise teams were fighting for

a place in the top four, none more so than Southampton, who claimed fourth place at Christmas following a 3-0 win over south coast rivals Portsmouth.

At the start of the new year, title rivals Man. United and Chelsea began to drop points, which allowed Arsenal to reclaim top spot in January. A run of nine consecutive wins followed, and the Gunners stayed at the summit for the rest of the season.

The title was sealed when Arsenal secured a 2-2 draw at White Hart Lane against Tottenham after second-placed Chelsea had lost at Newcastle. Their unbeaten campaign was rounded off with a 2-1 win over relegated Leicester at Highbury.

At the other end of the table, Leicester were joined in the Championship by Wolves and Leeds, whose 14-year stay in the Premier League came to an end.

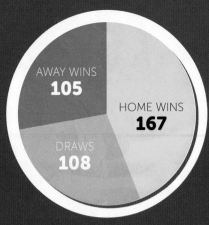

AWAY WINS
105

HOME WINS
167

DRAWS
108

GAMES PLAYED **380**

GOALS SCORED **1,012**

AVERAGE GOALS/GAME: **2.66**

TOP SCORERS

1. **Thierry Henry** — Arsenal — **30**
2. **Alan Shearer** — Newcastle — **22**
3. **=Louis Saha** — Man. United/Fulham — **20**
3. **=Ruud van Nistelrooy** — Man. United — **20**
5. **=Mikael Forssell** — Birmingham City — **16**
5. **=Juan Pablo Angel** — Aston Villa — **16**
5. **=Michael Owen** — Liverpool — **16**

PFA PLAYER OF THE YEAR:
Thierry Henry (Arsenal)

PFA YOUNG PLAYER OF THE YEAR:
Scott Parker (Charlton/Chelsea)

GOAL OF THE SEASON:
Dietmar Hamman, 17/03/04
Liverpool v Portsmouth

STATS

Biggest transfer:
£17m Damien Duff
(Blackburn to Chelsea)

Biggest win:
Portsmouth 6-1 Leeds

Longest winning run:
9 games (Arsenal)

Longest winless run:
14 games (Man. City)

Longest losing run:
6 games (Leeds)

Highest attendance:
67,758 (Man. United v Southampton)

Lowest attendance:
13,981 (Fulham v Blackburn)

Average attendance: 34,993

Longest Unbeaten Run:
38 games (Arsenal)

TEAM OF THE SEASON

Tim **Howard**

Lauren — Sol **Campbell** — John **Terry** — Ashley **Cole**

Steven **Gerrard** — Frank **Lampard** — Patrick **Vieira** — Robert **Pires**

Thierry **Henry** — Ruud **van Nistelrooy**

		P	W	D	L	F	A	GD	Pts
1	Arsenal	38	26	12	0	73	26	47	90
2	Chelsea	38	24	7	7	67	30	37	79
3	Man. United	38	23	6	9	64	35	29	75
4	Liverpool	38	16	12	10	55	37	18	60
5	Newcastle	38	13	17	8	52	40	12	56
6	Aston Villa	38	15	11	12	48	44	4	56
7	Charlton	38	14	11	13	51	51	0	53
8	Bolton	38	14	11	13	48	56	-8	53
9	Fulham	38	14	10	14	52	46	6	52
10	Birmingham	38	12	14	12	43	48	-5	50
11	Middlesbrough	38	13	9	16	44	52	-8	48
12	Southampton	38	12	11	15	44	45	-1	47
13	Portsmouth	38	12	9	17	47	54	-7	45
14	Tottenham	38	13	6	19	47	57	-10	45
15	Blackburn	38	12	8	18	51	59	-8	44
16	Man. City	38	9	14	15	55	54	+1	41
17	Everton	38	9	12	17	45	57	-12	39
18	Leicester	38	6	15	17	48	65	-17	33
19	Leeds	38	8	9	21	40	79	-39	33
20	Wolves	38	7	12	19	38	77	-39	33

2002-03

Manchester United came back from an eight-point deficit to topple defending Champions Arsenal and regain the Premier League, their eighth title win in ten years of the competition.

But it didn't look that way at the start of the season, as the Red Devils struggled to keep up with Arsène Wenger's Arsenal. Tottenham, the Gunners' North London rivals, also started the season strongly and topped the table after four games, but Arsenal won seven of their first nine to overtake their neighbours.

The Gunners finally lost their unbeaten start to the season when they travelled to Everton in October, in a game that will be remembered for the emergence of one of the Premier League's greatest players.

A 16-year-old Wayne Rooney came on as a substitute for Everton and won the game for the Toffees in the dying minutes. Picking the ball up halfway inside the Arsenal half, he crashed a curling, long-range

strike off the underside of David Seaman's crossbar to secure a 2-1 win for the home team.

A defeat to Blackburn soon followed for Arsenal, but they were back on top of the Premier League in November when they beat Tottenham 3-0 at Highbury. At that point the Gunners' nearest title rivals were Liverpool, who were unbeaten after 12 games, but an alarming slump saw them fail to win any of their next 11 matches and they slipped out of the top four.

That left Man. United and Chelsea as Arsenal's main rivals, but at the turn of the year the two teams trailed the Gunners by five points. That lead increased to eight points in March when Man. City beat United in the last Manchester derby at Maine Road, and the title race looked over.

But the Red Devils enjoyed a superb end to the season, and by the time they faced Arsenal at

Highbury on April 16 they were three points ahead of the Gunners, having played a game more.

The match ended 2-2, which preserved their three-point lead over Arsenal. United then went on to win their final four games, which meant that when Arsenal drew at Bolton and lost 3-2 at home to Leeds, the title was heading to Old Trafford for the eighth time in ten years.

The fight for safety went down to the last day of the season, where either Bolton or West Ham would join relegated West Brom and Sunderland. The two teams were equal on points, but Bolton's better goal difference gave them the advantage.

Ultimately, goal difference made no difference. Bolton beat Middlesbrough and West Ham could only draw with Birmingham, which consigned the Hammers to relegation with 42 points, the highest total for a relegated team.

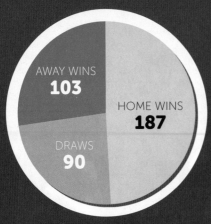

AWAY WINS
103

HOME WINS
187

DRAWS
90

GAMES PLAYED **380**
GOALS SCORED **1,000**

AVERAGE GOALS/GAME: **2.63**

TOP SCORERS

1. **Ruud van Nistelrooy** Man. United **23**
2. **Thierry Henry** Arsenal **24**
3. **James Beattie** Southampton **23**
4. **Mark Viduka** Leeds **20**
5. **Michael Owen** Liverpool **19**
6. **Alan Shearer** Newcastle **17**
7. **Nicolas Anelka** Man.City **15**

Longest winning run:
7 games (Liverpool)

STATS

Biggest transfer:
£34m Rio Ferdinand
(Leeds United to Man. United)

Biggest win:
West Brom 0-6 Liverpool

Longest unbeaten run:
18 games (Man. United)

Longest winless run:
20 games (Sunderland)

Longest losing run:
15 games (Sunderland)

Highest attendance:
67,721 (Man. United v Charlton)

Lowest attendance:
14,017 (Fulham v Blackburn)

Average attendance:
35,470

Brad **Friedel**

Stephen **Carr**

Sol **Campbell**

William **Gallas**

Ashley **Cole**

Robert **Pires**

Paul **Scholes**

Patrick **Vieira**

Kieron **Dyer**

Thierry **Henry**

Alan **Shearer**

TEAM OF THE SEASON

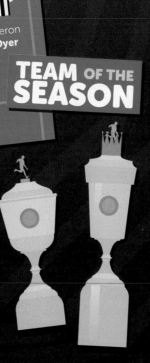

PFA PLAYER OF THE YEAR:
Thierry Henry (Arsenal)

PFA YOUNG PLAYER OF THE YEAR:
Jermaine Jenas (Newcastle)

GOAL OF THE SEASON:
Thierry Henry, 16/11/02
Arsenal v Tottenham

		P	W	D	L	F	A	GD	Pts
1	Man. United	38	25	8	5	74	34	40	83
2	Arsenal	38	23	9	6	85	42	43	78
3	Newcastle	38	21	6	11	63	48	15	69
4	Chelsea	38	19	10	9	68	38	30	67
5	Liverpool	38	18	10	10	61	41	20	64
6	Blackburn	38	16	12	10	52	43	9	60
7	Everton	38	17	8	13	48	49	-1	59
8	Southampton	38	13	13	12	43	46	-3	52
9	Man. City	38	15	6	17	47	54	-7	51
10	Tottenham	38	14	8	16	51	62	-11	50
11	Middlesbrough	38	13	10	15	48	44	4	49
12	Charlton	38	14	7	17	45	56	-11	49
13	Birmingham	38	13	9	16	41	49	-8	48
14	Fulham	38	13	9	16	41	50	-9	48
15	Leeds	38	14	5	19	58	57	1	47
16	Aston Villa	38	12	9	17	42	47	-5	45
17	Bolton	38	10	14	14	41	51	-10	44
18	West Ham	38	10	12	16	42	59	-17	42
19	WBA	38	6	8	24	29	65	-36	26
20	Sunderland	38	4	7	27	21	65	-44	19

2001-02

Arsenal ended three years of Man. United dominance by winning the 2001-02 Premier League, securing the title with a 1-0 win against their rivals at Old Trafford.

The summer of 2001 saw Frank Lampard move from West Ham to Chelsea for £11 million, Teddy Sheringham re-join Tottenham and Sol Campbell make the move across North London from Spurs to rivals Arsenal.

Leeds United, who had signed Republic Of Ireland striker Robbie Keane from Inter Milan, were the early-season pacesetters, and topped the League at the start of November after going on an 11- game unbeaten run. Liverpool and Aston Villa were their main rivals, with Villa goalkeeper Peter Schmeichel becoming the first goalkeeper to score in the Premier League when he found the net

late in a 2-1 defeat to Everton at Goodison Park.

By Christmas, Newcastle had taken over at the top of the table after beating Arsenal. Striker Alan Shearer, who would go on to become the first player to score 200 Premier League goals when he scored against Charlton, found the net 23 times that season.

After their defeat by Newcastle, Arsenal responded by going on a fantastic run that took them to the top of the Premier League, and despite pressure from Newcastle, Man. United, Leeds and Liverpool, the Gunners didn't lose another game all season.

Their penultimate game of the campaign was a trip to Old Trafford to face Man. United. The Red Devils knew they had to win to stand any chance of holding on to their title,

but Sylvain Wiltord's strike sealed a second Premier League title for Arsene Wenger's side.

They finished seven points ahead of second-placed Liverpool after winning their last 13 games. Arsene Wenger won the Manager Of The Season award, Robert Pires claimed the PFA Player Of The Year, and stalwarts Tony Adams and Lee Dixon announced their retirement.

Ipswich, who had finished fifth the previous season after gaining promotion, suffered relegation back to the Championship. The UEFA Cup took its toll on the side, who won only one of their first 17 games.

They were joined by Derby and Leicester, who said goodbye to their Filbert Street home after 111 years. That meant that all three promoted clubs – Blackburn, Bolton and Fulham – stayed up for the first time in Premier League history.

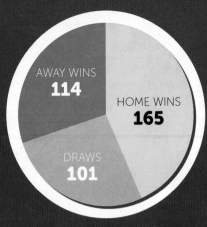

AWAY WINS **114**

HOME WINS **165**

DRAWS **101**

GAMES PLAYED 380
GOALS SCORED 1,001

AVERAGE GOALS/GAME: **2.61**

TOP SCORERS

1. **Thierry Henry** — **24**
   Arsenal

2. **=Alan Shearer** — **23**
   Newcastle

2. **=Jimmy Floyd Hasselbaink** — **23**
   Chelsea

2. **=Ruud van Nistelrooy** — **23**
   Man. United

5. **Michael Owen** — **19**
   Liverpool

6. **Ole Gunnar Solskjaer** — **17**
   Man. United

7. **Robbie Fowler** — **15**
   Liverpool/Leeds United

PFA PLAYER OF THE YEAR:
Ruud van Nistelrooy (Man. United)

PFA YOUNG PLAYER OF THE YEAR:
Craig Bellamy (Newcastle)

GOAL OF THE SEASON:
Dennis Bergkamp, 02/03/02
Newcastle v Arsenal

STATS

Biggest transfer:
£28m Juan Sebastian Veron
(Lazio to Man. United)

Biggest win:
Blackburn 7-1 West Ham

Longest winning run:
13 games (Arsenal)

Longest winless run:
16 games (Leicester)

Longest losing run:
7 games (Derby)

Highest attendance: 67,638
Man. (United v Middlesbrough)

Lowest attendance:
15,415 (Leicester v Middlesbrough)

Average attendance: 34,249

Longest Unbeaten Run:
21 games (Arsenal)

		P	W	D	L	F	A	GD	Pts
1	Arsenal (C)	38	26	9	3	79	36	43	87
2	Liverpool	38	24	8	6	67	30	37	80
3	Man.United	38	24	5	9	87	45	42	77
4	Newcastle	38	21	8	9	74	52	22	71
5	Leeds	38	18	12	8	53	37	16	66
6	Chelsea	38	17	13	8	66	38	28	64
7	West Ham	38	15	8	15	48	57	-9	53
8	Aston Villa	38	12	14	12	46	47	-1	50
9	Tottenham	38	14	8	16	49	53	-4	50
10	Blackburn	38	12	10	16	55	51	4	46
11	Southampton	38	12	9	17	46	54	-8	45
12	Middlesbrough	38	12	9	17	35	47	-12	45
13	Fulham	38	10	14	14	36	44	-8	44
14	Charlton	38	10	14	14	38	49	-11	44
15	Everton	38	11	10	17	45	57	-12	43
16	Bolton	38	9	13	16	44	62	-18	40
17	Sunderland	38	10	10	18	29	51	-22	40
18	Ipswich	38	9	9	20	41	64	-23	36
19	Derby	38	8	6	24	33	63	-30	30
20	Leicester	38	5	13	20	30	64	-34	28

TEAM OF THE SEASON

Shay **Given**

Steve **Finnan** — Rio **Ferdinand** — Sami **Hyypia** — Wayne **Bridge**

Robert **Pires** — Roy **Keane** — Patrick **Vieira** — Ryan **Giggs**

Thierry **Henry** — Ruud **van Nistelrooy**

2000-01

Manchester United claimed their seventh Premier League title in nine seasons, and in doing so became the first team to win three consecutive top-flight crowns since Liverpool in 1984.

Despite teams around them spending big to improve their squads in order to close the gap on United, the Red Devils' only major purchase was France's World Cup-winning goalkeeper, Fabien Barthez.

Chelsea bought Jimmy Floyd Hasselbaink and Eidur Gudjohnsen to spearhead their attack, but they only won one of their first five games and manager Gianluca Vialli was replaced by fellow Italian Claudio Ranieri.

Hasselbaink hit form and scored 23 Premier League goals, which was enough for him to win the Golden Boot, and the Blues recovered from their shaky start to finish sixth.

The early season pace-setters were Leicester City, who had won the League Cup the previous season. The Foxes were unbeaten in their first eight games, winning four and drawing four, and were top of the table when they took on second-placed Man. United at Filbert Street in October.

The game ended in a 3-0 win for United, and sparked a run of eight consecutive victories that saw them race clear at the top of the table, a position they wouldn't give up for the rest of the season.

A 6-1 win over Arsenal in February, which included a Dwight Yorke hat-trick, saw the Red Devils extend their lead over Arsenal to 16 points, who were in second place. They sealed the title in April, and despite losing the last three games of the season, still won the League by ten points.

Leeds, Liverpool and Ipswich battled it out for the third and final Champions League spot, and after the Yorkshire side beat the Reds at Anfield in April, they moved into third. However, the Reds went on to claim 19 points out of the next 21, which was just enough to regain the third and final Champions League place.

But possibly the story of the season was Ipswich. The Suffolk club, who had only won promotion the previous season, were battling for a Champions League spot for most of the season but eventually finished fifth, just three points adrift of third-placed Liverpool.

Man. City, who had won promotion the previous season along with Ipswich, fared differently, and suffered an instant return to the Championship. They were joined by Bradford and Coventry, who were relegated from the Premier League for the first time.

TOP SCORERS

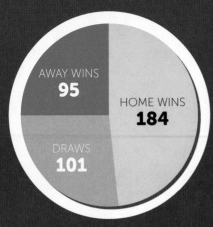

- AWAY WINS **95**
- HOME WINS **184**
- DRAWS **101**

GAMES PLAYED 380
GOALS SCORED 992

AVERAGE GOALS/GAME: **2.61**

1. **Jimmy Floyd Hasselbaink** — Leeds — **23**
2. **Marcus Stewart** — Ipswich Town — **19**
3. **=Thierry Henry** — Arsenal — **17**
3. **=Mark Viduka** — Leeds United — **17**
5. **Michael Owen** — Liverpool — **16**
6. **Teddy Sheringham** — Man. United — **15**
7. **=2 Players** — **14**

Longest losing run:
8 games (Leicester)

STATS

Biggest transfer:
£18m Rio Ferdinand
(West Ham to Leeds)

Biggest win:
Man. United 6-0 Bradford

Longest winning run:
8 games (Man. United)

Longest unbeaten run:
13 games (Leeds)

Longest winless run:
13 games (Bradford & Derby)

Highest attendance:
67,637 (Man. United v Coventry)

Lowest attendance:
15,523 (Bradford v Coventry)

Average attendance: 32,905

TEAM OF THE SEASON

Fabien **Barthez**

Stephen **Carr** — Jaap **Stam** — Wes **Brown** — **Sylvinho**

Steven **Gerrard** — Roy **Keane** — Patrick **Vieira** — Ryan **Giggs**

Thierry **Henry** — Teddy **Sheringham**

PFA PLAYER OF THE YEAR:
Teddy Sheringham (Man. United)

PFA YOUNG PLAYER OF THE YEAR:
Steven Gerrard (Liverpool)

GOAL OF THE SEASON:
Shaun Bartlett, 01/04/01
Charlton v Leicester City

		P	W	D	L	F	A	GD	Pts
1	Man.United	38	24	8	6	79	31	48	80
2	Arsenal	38	20	10	8	63	38	25	70
3	Liverpool	38	20	9	9	71	39	32	69
4	Leeds	38	20	8	10	64	43	21	68
5	Ipswich	38	20	6	12	57	42	15	66
6	Chelsea	38	17	10	11	68	45	23	61
7	Sunderland	38	15	12	11	46	41	5	57
8	Aston Villa	38	13	15	10	46	43	3	54
9	Charlton	38	14	10	14	50	57	-7	52
10	Southampton	38	14	10	14	40	48	-8	52
11	Newcastle	38	14	9	15	44	50	-6	51
12	Tottenham	38	13	10	15	47	54	-7	49
13	Leicester	38	14	6	18	39	51	-12	48
14	Middlesbrough	38	9	15	14	44	44	0	42
15	West Ham	38	10	12	16	45	50	-5	42
16	Everton	38	11	9	18	45	59	-14	42
17	Derby	38	10	12	16	37	59	-22	42
18	Man. City	38	8	10	20	41	65	-24	34
19	Coventry	38	8	10	20	36	63	-27	34
20	Bradford	38	5	11	22	30	70	-40	26

THE
90's

1999-00

A year after winning a historic treble, Manchester United claimed their sixth Premier League title in eight seasons, breaking a number of records along the way.

The Red Devils not only scored a record 97 Premier League goals, more than any other club in any season, but they also won the title by a record-breaking 18-point margin.

A run of 11 successive wins at the end of the season sealed the Premier League title, but their title defence looked far from assured when a number of their rivals strengthened their squads considerably before the start of the season.

Arsenal, who had finished just a point behind United the previous season, replaced Real Madrid-bound Nicolas Anelka with fellow countryman and 1998 World Cup winner Thierry Henry, who joined

the club from Juventus.

It took the Frenchman eight games to score his first goal for the club, a superb strike at Southampton, but he still went on to score a admirable 17 Premier League goals in his first season.

After Man. United had led the table during the early part of the season, a shock 5-0 defeat at the hands of Chelsea at Stamford Bridge saw Leeds take top spot.

The Yorkshire club had an exciting young team under manager David O'Leary, and were inspired by young Australian winger Harry Kewell, who went on to win the PFA Young Player Of The Year.

A run of 12 wins in 14 games saw O'Leary's team top the Premier League at Christmas, with Man. United second and Arsenal third. United regained top spot at the end of January and only lost one

more game all season, a 3-0 defeat against Newcastle at St. James' Park.

Following that defeat, United won one and drew two of their next three games, before an 11-game winning streak saw them claim their sixth Premier League title in style.

Arsenal finished second, while Leeds finished third to earn Champions League qualification at the expense of Liverpool. The Reds suffered a shock final-day defeat at the hands of Bradford, whose victory ensured their Premier League survival.

At the other end of the table, Bradford's dramatic win over Liverpool condemned Wimbledon to join relegated Sheffield Wednesday and Watford in the Championship for the 2001-02 season.

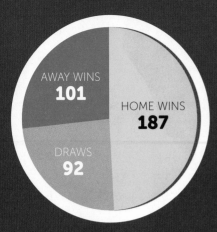

AWAY WINS **101**

HOME WINS **187**

DRAWS **92**

GAMES PLAYED **380**

GOALS SCORED **1,060**

AVERAGE GOALS/GAME: **2.79**

TOP SCORERS

1. **Kevin Phillips** Sunderland — **30**
2. **Alan Shearer** Newcastle — **23**
3. **Dwight Yorke** Man. United — **20**
4. **=Michael Bridges** Leeds United — **19**
4. **=Andy Cole** Man. United — **19**
6. **Thierry Henry** Arsenal — **17**
7. **Paolo Di Canio** West Ham — **16**

Longest winless run: 11 games (Sunderland & Watford)

STATS

Biggest transfer: £11m Emile Heskey (Leicester to Liverpool)

Biggest win: Newcastle 8-0 Sheff. Wed.

Longest winning run: 11 games (Man. United)

Longest unbeaten run: 16 games (Chelsea)

Longest winless run: Longest losing run: 8 games (Wimbledon)

Highest attendance: 61,619 (Man. United v Derby)

Lowest attendance: 8,248 (Wimbledon v Sheff. Wed.)

Average attendance: 30,755

Nigel **Martyn**

Gary **Kelly** · Jaap **Stam** · Sami **Hyypia** · Ian **Harte**

David **Beckham** · Roy **Keane** · Patrick **Vieira** · Harry **Kewell**

Andy **Cole** · Kevin **Phillips**

TEAM OF THE SEASON

PFA PLAYER OF THE YEAR: Roy Keane (Man. United)

PFA YOUNG PLAYER OF THE YEAR: Harry Kewell (Leeds)

GOAL OF THE SEASON: Pablo Di Canio, 26/03/00 West Ham v Wimbledon

		P	W	D	L	F	A	GD	Pts
1	Man.United	38	28	7	3	97	45	52	91
2	Arsenal	38	22	7	9	73	43	30	73
3	Leeds United	38	21	6	11	58	43	15	69
4	Liverpool	38	19	10	9	51	30	21	67
5	Chelsea	38	18	11	9	53	34	19	65
6	Aston Villa	38	15	13	10	46	35	11	58
7	Sunderland	38	16	10	12	57	56	1	58
8	Leicester	38	16	7	15	55	55	0	55
9	West Ham	38	15	10	13	52	53	-1	55
10	Tottenham	38	15	8	15	57	49	8	53
11	Newcastle	38	14	10	14	63	54	9	52
12	Middlesbrough	38	14	10	14	46	52	-6	52
13	Everton	38	12	14	12	59	49	10	50
14	Coventry	38	12	8	18	47	54	-7	44
15	Southampton	38	12	8	18	45	62	-17	44
16	Derby	38	9	11	18	44	57	-13	38
17	Bradford	38	9	9	20	38	68	-30	36
18	Wimbledon	38	7	12	19	46	74	-28	33
19	Sheff. Wed.	38	8	7	23	38	70	-32	31
20	Watford	38	6	6	26	35	77	-42	24

1998-99

Manchester United were crowned Premier League champions again but, more significantly, put their name in the history books by becoming the first ever English club to win the League, FA Cup and Champions League in the same season.

An incredible year was sealed during an amazing ten day spell in May 1999, with the Premier League the first of the three trophies secured. United came from behind on the final day of the season to beat Tottenham 2-1, with rivals Arsenal finishing just one point behind.

Following an impressive World Cup, 18-year-old England striker Michael Owen continued where he'd left off by scoring a hat-trick on the first day of the season.

The striker went on to score 18 goals and shared the Golden Boot with Leeds' Jimmy Floyd Hasselbaink and Dwight Yorke, who shone at Man. United after joining from Aston Villa for £12.6million.

Villa made up for the loss of Yorke by signing Dion Dublin from Coventry and Paul Merson from Arsenal, and they starred for the Villans. The club spent the first half of the season at the top of the table, but a 10-match winless run at the turn of the year put paid to their title hopes.

Villa's poor form and a difficult winter for Leeds meant that the title race was played out by Man. United, Arsenal and Chelsea. After losing their opening game of the season at Coventry, Chelsea went on a 22-game unbeaten run to put them firmly in the title frame.

At the turn of the new year, Man. United won five games on the trot to move to the top of the table. These included a 6-2 win at Leicester and an 8-1 victory at Nottingham Forest, where Ole Gunnar Solskjaer came on as a substitute and scored four goals in the last ten minutes.

The Red Devils didn't lose again all

season, but only one defeat each for Arsenal and Chelsea meant the title went to the wire. On the last day, the Gunners were one point behind United. Arsenal beat Aston Villa 1-0, but United came back from 1-0 down to beat Tottenham 2-1, and the first part of the treble was secured.

The relegation fight was just as dramatic. Both Southampton and Everton had amazing run-ins to avoid relegation. The Toffees won four of their last six matches, while Southampton climbed out of the relegation zone for the first time all season in May.

The Saints' final day win over Everton meant Charlton were relegated after their first Premier League season. They were joined by Blackburn, who had won the title just four years earlier, and Nottingham Forest, who finished bottom.

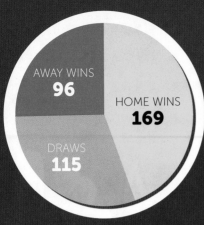

AWAY WINS
96

HOME WINS
169

DRAWS
115

GAMES PLAYED **380**

GOALS SCORED **963**

AVERAGE GOALS/GAME: **2.53**

TOP SCORERS

1. **Jimmy Floyd Hasselbaink** — Leeds — **18**

1. **=Michael Owen** — Liverpool — **18**

1. **=Dwight Yorke** — Man. United — **18**

4. **=Nicolas Anelka** — Arsenal — **17**

4. **=Andy Cole** — Man. United — **17**

6. **Hamilton Ricard** — Middlesbrough — **15**

7. **=4 Players** — **14**

PFA PLAYER OF THE YEAR:
David Ginola (Tottenham)

PFA YOUNG PLAYER OF THE YEAR:
Nicolas Anelka (Arsenal)

GOAL OF THE SEASON:
Ryan Giggs, 14/04/99
Man. United v Arsenal (FA Cup)

STATS

Biggest transfer:
£12.6m Dwight Yorke
(Aston Villa to Man. United)

Biggest win:
Nott'm Forest 1-8 Man. United

Longest winning run:
7 games (Leeds)

Longest unbeaten run:
21 games (Chelsea)

Longest winless run:
19 games (Nott'm Forest)

Longest losing run:
8 games (Charlton)

Lowest attendance:
11,717 (Wimbledon v Coventry)

Average attendance: 30,591

Highest attendance:
44,619 (Liverpool v Everton)

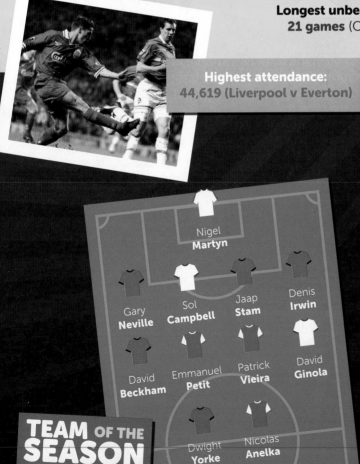

TEAM OF THE SEASON

Nigel **Martyn**

Gary **Neville** — Sol **Campbell** — Jaap **Stam** — Denis **Irwin**

David **Beckham** — Emmanuel **Petit** — Patrick **Vieira** — David **Ginola**

Dwight **Yorke** — Nicolas **Anelka**

		P	W	D	L	F	A	GD	Pts
1	Man. United	38	22	13	3	80	37	43	79
2	Arsenal	38	22	12	4	59	17	42	78
3	Chelsea	38	20	15	3	57	30	27	75
4	Leeds	38	18	13	7	62	34	28	67
5	West Ham	38	16	9	13	46	53	-7	57
6	Aston Villa	38	15	10	13	51	46	5	55
7	Liverpool	38	15	9	14	68	49	19	54
8	Derby	38	13	13	12	40	45	-5	52
9	Middlesbrough	38	12	15	11	48	54	-6	51
10	Leicester	38	12	13	13	40	46	-6	49
11	Tottenham	38	11	14	13	47	50	-3	47
12	Sheff. Wed.	38	13	7	18	41	42	-1	46
13	Newcastle	38	11	13	14	48	54	-6	46
14	Everton	38	11	10	17	42	47	-5	43
15	Coventry	38	11	9	18	39	51	-12	42
16	Wimbledon	38	10	12	16	40	63	-23	42
17	Southampton	38	11	8	19	37	64	-27	41
18	Charlton	38	8	12	18	41	56	-15	36
19	Blackburn	38	7	14	17	38	52	-14	35
20	Nott'm Forest	38	7	9	22	35	69	-34	30

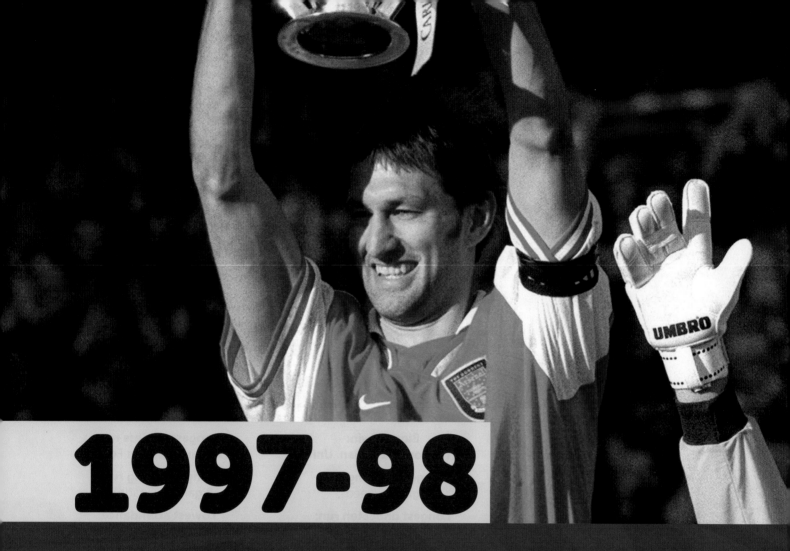

1997-98

In his first full season as Arsenal manager, Arsene Wenger led Arsenal to their first Premier League title, and their first top-flight title since 1991. The Gunners also lifted the FA Cup to cap an incredible season for the North London side.

The title had seemed unlikely at Christmas for Arsenal, but an incredible run of 45 points from a possible 51 in the second half of the season saw the Gunners beat rivals Manchester United by a single point.

Newcastle United, who had finished second in the previous two campaigns, struggled to replicate that form under Kenny Dalglish and the Magpies eventually finished 13th.

But it was Dalglish's old side, Blackburn, who were the early season pace-setters, with Roy Hodgson leading his new club to four wins from the first five games.

They couldn't maintain the form all the way through until Christmas, but were still looking strong in second place by the time the festive period arrived.

There was a familiar look about the table at Christmas as it was Man. United who sat at the top, helped by a run of six consecutive wins following a 3-2 defeat to Arsenal. The Gunners themselves had slipped to sixth place, 13 points behind the Red Devils, but their title charge was soon to begin.

By as late as the beginning of March, United were still 12 points ahead of Arsenal, but had played three more games than their London rivals. When the two clubs met at Old Trafford on March 14, Arsenal came away with a 1-0 win, and it turned the title race on its head.

The Gunners won ten games on the trot to win the Premier League, which was sealed with a 4-0 win at home to Everton. Arsenal even lost the last two games of the season, against Liverpool and Aston Villa, as they looked to rest players ahead of the FA Cup final.

London rivals Tottenham were in the relegation zone at the turn of the year, but the return of striker Jurgen Klinsmann, who had impressed so much in his first spell at the club, helped turn their fortunes around. The Germany star hit nine goals in 15 matches to ensure the club finished in 14th place.

The battle at the bottom of the table was left between Everton and the three promoted clubs, Bolton, Crystal Palace and Barnsley. Palace and Barnsley had already been relegated by the final day of the season and Everton stayed up in dramatic fashion, meaning all three promoted teams suffered an instant return to the Championship.

AWAY WINS **101**

HOME WINS **184**

DRAWS **95**

GAMES PLAYED 380

GOALS SCORED 1,018

AVERAGE GOALS/GAME: **2.68**

TOP SCORERS

1. **Dion Dublin** — Coventry City — **18**
1. **=Michael Owen** — Liverpool — **18**
1. **=Chris Sutton** — Blackburn Rovers — **18**
4. **=Dennis Bergkamp** — Arsenal — **16**
4. **=Kevin Gallagher** — Blackburn Rovers — **16**
4. **=Jimmy Floyd Hasselbaink** — Leeds United — **16**
7. **=2 Players** — **15**

Longest winless run:
15 games (Crystal Palace)

STATS

Biggest transfer:
£5m Graeme Le Saux
(Blackburn to Chelsea)

Biggest win:
Man. United 7-0 Barnsley

Longest winning run:
10 games (Arsenal)

Longest unbeaten run:
18 games (Arsenal)

Longest losing run:
8 games (Crystal Palace)

Highest attendance: 55,306
Man. United v Wimbledon

Lowest attendance: 7,668
Wimbledon v Barnsley

Average attendance: 29,212

Nigel **Martyn**

Gary **Neville** — Gary **Pallister** — Colin **Hendry** — Graeme **Le Saux**

David **Beckham** — Nicky **Butt** — David **Batty** — Ryan **Giggs**

Michael **Owen** — Dennis **Bergkamp**

TEAM OF THE SEASON

PFA PLAYER OF THE YEAR:
Dennis Bergkamp (Arsenal)

PFA YOUNG PLAYER OF THE YEAR:
Michael Owen (Liverpool)

GOAL OF THE SEASON:
Dennis Bergkamp, 27/08/97
Leicester v Arsenal

		P	W	D	L	F	A	GD	Pts
1	Arsenal	38	23	9	6	68	33	35	78
2	Man.United	38	23	8	7	73	26	47	77
3	Liverpool	38	18	11	9	68	42	26	65
4	Chelsea	38	20	3	15	71	43	28	63
5	Leeds	38	17	8	13	57	46	11	59
6	Blackburn	38	16	10	12	57	52	5	58
7	Aston Villa	38	17	6	15	49	48	1	57
8	West Ham	38	16	8	14	56	57	-1	56
9	Derby	38	16	7	15	52	49	3	55
10	Leicester	38	13	14	11	51	41	10	53
11	Coventry	38	12	16	10	46	44	2	52
12	Southampton	38	14	6	18	50	55	-5	48
13	Newcastle	38	11	11	16	35	44	-9	44
14	Tottenham	38	11	11	16	44	56	-12	44
15	Wimbledon	38	10	14	14	34	46	-12	44
16	Sheff Wed.	38	12	8	18	52	67	-15	44
17	Everton	38	9	13	16	41	56	-15	40
18	Bolton	38	9	13	16	41	61	-20	40
19	Barnsley	38	10	5	23	37	82	-45	35
20	Crystal Palace	38	8	9	21	37	71	-34	33

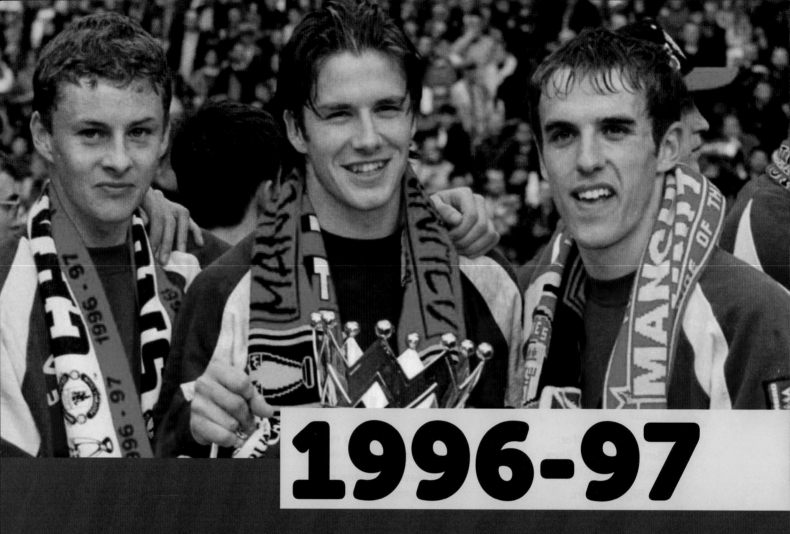

1996-97

Man. United secured their fourth Premier League title in five seasons, finishing seven points ahead of second-placed Newcastle, who were runners-up for the second consecutive season.

The Magpies, who had let a 12-point lead slip to allow United to win the title in 1996-97, showed their intent by breaking the world transfer record to sign England striker Alan Shearer from Blackburn for £15 million.

After two defeats from their first three games, Newcastle won the next six before welcoming Man. United to St. James' Park in October. The home side were in scintillating form, hammering the champions 5-0, and a subsequent 6-3 defeat to Southampton and a 2-1 reverse against Chelsea set alarm bells ringing around Old Trafford.

But United then went on a 16-game unbeaten run, starting with a 1-0 win over Arsenal, who had appointed Nagoya Grampus Eight manager Arsene Wenger the previous month. Key to the The Red Devils' resurgence was Eric Cantona, who scored a sublime chip in the 5-0 thrashing of Sunderland at Old Trafford. No-one knew then that this would be the last season they would see the French striker, as he announced his retirement at the end of the season at the age of just 30.

Newcastle's title hopes were dealt a blow when a seven-game winless run saw them slip to sixth, and despite a 7-1 win over Tottenham in the following match, manager Kevin Keegan shocked the club by resigning.

He was replaced by former Blackburn manager Kenny Dalglish, whose arrival saw the Magpies fight their way back into the title race. However, another 4-3 defeat at Anfield put an end to any realistic title ambitions. It was confirmed with two games to spare as Newcastle drew away at West Ham, meaning United were champions again.

With the title race decided, attention turned to the battle against relegation. Nottingham Forest were already down but Southampton, who had been five points adrift of safety, embarked on a seven-game unbeaten run to all but ensure their survival.

That left Middlesbrough and Coventry looking to overtake 17th placed Sunderland to secure their safety on the last day of the season. Boro, who had been deducted three points for failing to fulfil a fixture against Blackburn due to illness and injury, could only manage a 1-1 draw at Leeds and were relegated. They were joined by Sunderland, after Coventry won 2-1 at Tottenham and the Black Cats suffered a 1-0 defeat at Wimbledon.

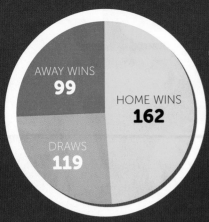

AWAY WINS **99**

HOME WINS **162**

DRAWS **119**

GAMES PLAYED 380

GOALS SCORED 970

AVERAGE GOALS/GAME: **2.55**

TOP SCORERS

1. **Alan Shearer**
   Newcastle United **25**

2. **Ian Wright**
   Arsenal **23**

3. **=Robbie Fowler**
   Liverpool **18**

3. **=Ole Gunnar Solskjaer**
   Man. United **18**

5. **Dwight Yorke**
   Aston Villa **17**

6. **=Les Ferdinand**
   Newcastle **16**

7. **=Fabrizio Ravanelli**
   Middlesbrough **16**

PFA PLAYER OF THE YEAR:
Alan Shearer (Newcastle)

PFA YOUNG PLAYER OF THE YEAR:
David Beckham (Man. United)

GOAL OF THE SEASON:
Trevor Sinclair, 25/01/97
QPR v Barnsley

STATS

Biggest transfer:
£15m Alan Shearer
(Blackburn to Newcastle)

Longest winning run:
7 games (Newcastle)

Longest unbeaten run:
16 games (Man. United)

Longest winless run:
16 games (Nott'm Forest)

Longest losing run:
6 games (Everton)

Highest attendance:
55,314 (Man. United v Wimbledon)

Lowest Attendance:
7,979 (Wimbledon v Leeds)

Average attendance: XXX

Biggest win:
Everton 7-1 Southampton &
Newcastle 7-1 Tottenham

David **Seaman**

Gary **Neville**   Tony **Adams**   Mark **Wright**   Stig Inge **Bjornebye**

David **Beckham**   Roy **Keane**   David **Batty**   Steve **McManaman**

Alan **Shearer**   Ian **Wright**

TEAM OF THE SEASON

		P	W	D	L	F	A	GD	Pts
1	Man. United	38	21	12	5	76	44	32	75
2	Newcastle	38	19	11	8	73	40	33	68
3	Arsenal	38	19	11	8	62	32	30	68
4	Liverpool	38	19	11	8	62	37	25	68
5	Aston Villa	38	17	10	11	47	34	13	61
6	Chelsea	38	16	11	11	58	55	3	59
7	Shef. Wed.	38	14	15	9	50	51	-1	57
8	Wimbledon	38	15	11	12	49	46	3	56
9	Leicester	38	12	11	15	46	54	-8	47
10	Tottenham	38	13	7	18	44	51	-7	46
11	Leeds	38	11	13	14	28	38	-10	46
12	Derby	38	11	13	14	45	58	-13	46
13	Blackburn	38	9	15	14	42	43	-1	42
14	West Ham	38	10	12	16	39	48	-9	42
15	Everton	38	10	12	16	44	57	-13	42
16	Southampton	38	10	11	17	50	56	-6	41
17	Coventry	38	9	14	15	38	54	-16	41
18	Sunderland	38	10	10	18	35	53	-18	40
19	Middlesbrough	38	10	12	16	51	60	-9	39
20	Nott'm Forest	38	6	16	16	31	59	-28	34

1995-96

After giving up their Premier League crown to Blackburn the previous season, many experts predicted a powerful response from Man. United. But instead of bringing in expensive reinforcements, they let experienced first-team trio Mark Hughes, Paul Ince and Andrei Kanchelskis leave the club without bringing in replacements.

Instead, Alex Ferguson brought through a number of academy stars into his squad. After a 3-1 opening day defeat at Aston Villa some were questioning his wisdom, but they recovered from being 12 points behind Newcastle at one stage to clinch their third Premier League title.

Following the defeat at Villa, United won their next five games and then in October, welcomed back talismanic striker Eric Cantona after his nine-month ban. But, by this time Newcastle had surged ahead to the top of the Premier League.

Boosted by the signings of Les Ferdinand from QPR and French winger David Ginola, the Magpies won nine of their opening ten games.

The first meeting between leaders Newcastle and nearest challengers Man. United came on December 27 at Old Trafford, with Ferguson's side coming out on top. Five successive victories followed for Newcastle, and at one stage they were 12 points clear of their nearest rivals. However, a slump of four defeats in six matches, including a narrow defeat to Man. United, saw Alex Ferguson's team claim top spot. The Magpies spent 212 days at the summit, the most in Premier League history for a side not crowned as champions.

On April 3, Newcastle travelled to Liverpool. Keegan's side went 3-2 ahead just before the hour mark, but two late Collymore goals, including one in stoppage time, clinched a 4-3 victory for the Reds.

That left Man. United three points clear, although Newcastle had one match in hand, and a 3-2 victory at rivals Man. City stretched that lead the following weekend.

A 3-1 defeat at Southampton was the only time United dropped points for the rest of the season. Newcastle's draw with Nottingham Forest a couple of weeks later handed the title to Old Trafford for the third time in four years, this time by a winning margin of four points.

The relegation battle went down to the wire, with Southampton, Coventry City and Man. City all level on points going into the final day, battling to avoid joining Bolton and QPR. Man. City eventually went down on goal difference. Needing to better goalless draws for Southampton and Coventry, City rallied from 2-0 down against Liverpool to level at 2-2 with 12 minutes left but couldn't find a third.

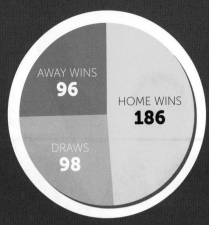

AWAY WINS
96

HOME WINS
186

DRAWS
98

GAMES PLAYED **380**

GOALS SCORED **988**

AVERAGE GOALS/GAME: **2.60**

TOP SCORERS

1. **Alan Shearer** Blackburn Rovers **31**

2. **Robbie Fowler** Liverpool **28**

3. **Les Ferdinand** QPR **25**

4. **Dwight Yorke** Aston Villa **17**

5. **=Andrei Kanchelskis** Everton **16**

5. **=Teddy Sheringham** Tottenham **16**

7. **=2 Players** **15**

Longest unbeaten run:
15 games (Liverpool)

STATS

Biggest transfer:
£8.4m Stan Collymore
(Nott'm Forest to Liverpool)

Biggest win:
Blackburn 7-0 Nott'm Forest

Longest winning run:
6 games (Man. United)

Longest winless run:
14 games (Coventry & Wimbledon)

Longest losing run:
8 games (Man. City & Middlesbrough)

Highest attendance:
53,926 (Man. United v Nott'm Forest)

Lowest Attendance:
6,352 (Wimbledon v Sheff. Wed.)

Average attendance: XXX

David **James**

Gary **Neville**　Tony **Adams**　Ugo **Ehiogu**　Alan **Wright**

Steve **Stone**　Rob **Lee**　Ruud **Gullit**　David **Ginola**

Alan **Shearer**　Les **Ferdinand**

TEAM OF THE **SEASON**

PFA PLAYER OF THE YEAR:
Les Ferdinand (Newcastle)

PFA YOUNG PLAYER OF THE YEAR:
Robbie Fowler (Liverpool)

GOAL OF THE SEASON:
Tony Yeboah, 23/09/95
Wimbledon v Leeds

		P	W	D	L	F	A	GD	Pts
1	Man. United	38	25	7	6	73	35	38	82
2	Newcastle	38	24	6	8	66	37	29	78
3	Liverpool	38	20	11	7	70	34	36	71
4	Aston Villa	38	18	9	11	52	35	17	63
5	Arsenal	38	17	12	9	49	32	17	63
6	Everton	38	17	10	11	64	44	20	61
7	Blackburn	38	18	7	13	61	47	14	61
8	Tottenham	38	16	13	9	50	38	12	61
9	Nott'm Forest	38	15	13	10	50	54	-4	58
10	West Ham	38	14	9	15	43	52	-9	51
11	Chelsea	38	12	14	12	46	44	2	50
12	Middlesbrough	38	11	10	17	35	50	-15	43
13	Leeds	38	12	7	19	40	57	-17	43
14	Wimbledon	38	10	11	17	55	70	-15	41
15	Sheff. Wed.	38	10	10	18	48	61	-13	40
16	Coventry	38	8	14	16	42	60	-18	38
17	Southampton	38	9	11	18	34	52	-18	38
18	Man. City	38	9	11	18	33	58	-25	38
19	QPR	38	9	6	23	38	57	-19	33
20	Bolton	38	8	5	25	39	71	-32	29

1994-95

Blackburn Rovers, who had only been promoted back to the top flight two seasons earlier, ended their 81-year wait for a top-flight title. Kenny Dalglish's side finished one point ahead of Man. United, who themselves were aiming for a hat-trick of title wins, claiming the title on the last day of the season.

Rovers' title charge was spearheaded by Alan Shearer and Chris Sutton, dubbed the 'SAS', who hit 49 league goals between them. Shearer's 34 goals earned him the Golden Boot and equalled Andy Cole's League-high tally of 34 goals from the previous campaign, while Sutton hit 15 goals after his record-breaking £5 million summer move from Norwich.

Newcastle started the season strongest, going the first 11 games unbeaten before losing 2-0 to Man. United. Their star man was 22-year-old Andrew Cole, who would join the Red Devils in a record £6 million deal in January 1995 to add to United's already impressive forward line.

But it was Blackburn who took top spot off Newcastle with a run of seven consecutive victories. They went on to win four of the next five, but their unbeaten run was ended with a 1-0 defeat to Man. United at Old Trafford. Eric Cantona scored the winner, but his Premier League season came to an end just a few days later at Crystal Palace. After being sent off at Selhurst Park, he was involved in an altercation with a fan as he walked off and was subsequently banned for nine months. The Red Devils felt his absence, losing at Everton and Liverpool and dropping costly points against Tottenham, Leeds and Chelsea.

By the last day of the season, United trailed Blackburn by two points. Rovers had a tricky trip to Anfield to face Liverpool, while Man. United travelled to West Ham. Alan Shearer put Blackburn ahead at Anfield, and when Michael Hughes gave West Ham the lead against United, it looked like the

title was heading to Ewood Park. But Brian McClair equalised for United before strikes from John Barnes and Jamie Redknapp gave Liverpool a 2-1 lead, meaning United needed just one more goal to claim top spot.

West Ham keeper Ludek Miklosko had an outstanding game and kept United at bay. Blackburn, despite losing, claimed the title and celebrated on the pitch, along with many Liverpool fans in the stands, who were delighted their arch-rivals had been denied. United finished one point behind Blackburn and Nottingham Forest, who had only been promoted that season, finished third.

At the other end of the table, Crystal Palace and Leicester suffered immediate returns to the Championship along with Norwich, who only two seasons earlier had made the Champions League places.

Pie chart

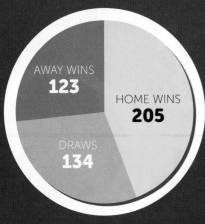

AWAY WINS **123**
HOME WINS **205**
DRAWS **134**

GAMES PLAYED **462**
GOALS SCORED **1,195**
AVERAGE GOALS/GAME: **2.59**

TOP SCORERS

1. **Alan Shearer** Blackburn Rovers — **34**
2. **Robbie Fowler** Liverpool — **25**
3. **Les Ferdinand** QPR — **24**
4. **Stan Collymore** Nottingham Forest — **22**
5. **= Andy Cole** Man. Utd./Newcastle — **21**
5. **= Jurgen Klinsmann** Tottenham — **21**
7. **Matt Le Tissier** Southampton — **19**

PFA PLAYER OF THE YEAR:
Alan Shearer (Blackburn)

PFA YOUNG PLAYER OF THE YEAR:
Robbie Fowler (Liverpool)

GOAL OF THE SEASON:
Matt Le Tissier, 10/12/94
Blackburn v Southampton

STATS

Biggest transfer:
£7m Andy Cole
(Newcastle United to Man. United)

Longest winning run:
7 games (Blackburn)

Longest unbeaten run:
13 games (Nott'm Forest)

Longest winless run:
12 games (Everton & Southampton)

Longest losing run:
8 games (Ipswich)

Highest attendance:
43,868 (Man. United v Sheff. Wed.)

Lowest Attendance:
5,268 (Wimbledon v Man. City)

Average attendance: XXX

Biggest win:
Man. United 9-0 Ipswich

TEAM OF THE SEASON

Tim **Flowers**

Rob **Jones** — Gary **Pallister** — Colin **Hendry** — Graeme **Le Saux**

Matt **Le Tissier** — Paul **Ince** — Tim **Sherwood**

Jurgen **Klinsmann** — Alan **Shearer** — Chris **Sutton**

League table

		P	W	D	L	F	A	GD	Pts
1	Blackburn	42	27	8	7	80	39	41	89
2	Man. United	42	26	10	6	77	28	49	88
3	Nott'm Forest	42	22	11	9	72	43	29	77
4	Liverpool	42	21	11	10	65	37	28	74
5	Leeds	42	20	13	9	59	38	21	73
6	Newcastle	42	20	12	10	67	47	20	72
7	Tottenham	42	16	14	12	66	58	8	62
8	QPR	42	17	9	16	61	59	2	60
9	Wimbledon	42	15	11	16	48	65	-17	56
10	Southampton	42	12	18	12	61	63	-2	54
11	Chelsea	42	13	15	14	50	55	-5	54
12	Arsenal	42	13	12	17	52	49	3	51
13	Sheff. Wed.	42	13	12	17	49	57	-8	51
14	West Ham	42	13	11	18	44	48	-4	50
15	Everton	42	11	17	14	44	51	-7	50
16	Coventry	42	12	14	16	44	62	-18	50
17	Man. City	42	12	13	17	53	64	-11	49
18	Aston Villa	42	11	15	16	51	56	-5	48
19	Crystal Palace	42	11	12	19	34	49	-15	45
20	Norwich	42	10	13	19	37	54	-17	43
21	Leicester	42	6	11	25	45	80	-35	29
22	Ipswich	42	7	6	29	36	93	-57	27

1993-94

After ending a 26-year wait for the title the previous season, Manchester United secured their second consecutive Premier League title win in 1993-94. The Red Devils were top of the League for most of the campaign, and ended up winning the title by eight points to second-placed Blackburn. Success in the FA Cup secured the double for Alex Ferguson's side, and in doing so they became only the fourth teamin the 20th century to achieve the feat.

United faced Aston Villa and Norwich early in the campaign, who had finished second and third respectively the previous season. A 2-0 win at Norwich on the opening day was followed by a 2-1 victory at Villa eight days later, a result which took United top.

Despite defeat to United, Norwich were among the early challengers, and Canaries striker Efan Ekoku became the first striker to score four goals in a Premier League

match as they beat Everton 5-1 at Goodison Park.

But that was about as good as things got for Norwich. Their form tailed off dramatically from November and they finished the season in 13th place, leaving Newcastle and Blackburn as Man. United's two main title rivals.

Man. United's only defeat before the start of 1994 came at Chelsea, after which they went on a 22-game unbeaten run before the Blues beat them again at Old Trafford on March 5. A slight dip in form allowed Kenny Dalglish's Blackburn to close the gap. Boosted by the arrivals of goalkeeper Tim Flowers in November and Ian Pearce and David Batty the previous month,

Rovers won 16 out of 20 matches from December until mid-April. The run included a 2-0 victory against Man. United, which reduced the Red Devils' advantage to three points at the top.

But a relentless and dogged United side won five out of their last seven games, while Balckburn stuttered and won only one out of their final five matches. Rovers' 2-1 defeat at Coventry sealed the title for United, who ensured the Premier League title remained at Old Trafford. The Red Devils finished eight points ahead of Blackburn, with Newcastle finishing third and Arsenal in fourth place.

The scrap for Premier League survival was tense and went to the final day of the season. Everton, who had enjoyed an unbroken 40 years in the top flight, beat Wimbledon 3-2 to maintain their Premier League status, meaning Sheffield United and Oldham joined bottom club Swindon, who conceded a Premier League-record 100 goals in the season.

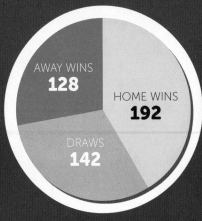

AWAY WINS **128**

HOME WINS **192**

DRAWS **142**

GAMES PLAYED **462**

GOALS SCORED **1,195**

AVERAGE GOALS/GAME: **2.59**

TOP SCORERS

1. **Andy Cole** — Newcastle United — **34**
2. **Alan Shearer** — Blackburn Rovers — **31**
3. = **Matt Le Tissier** — Southampton — **25**
3. = **Chris Sutton** — Norwich City — **25**
5. **Ian Wright** — Arsenal — **20**
6. **Peter Beardsley** — Newcastle United — **19**
7. **Mark Bright** — Sheffield Wednesday — **18**

STATS

Biggest transfer:
£3.75m Roy Keane
(Nottingham Forest To Man. United)

Biggest win:
Newcastle 7-1 Swindon

Longest winning run:
8 games (Man. United)

Longest unbeaten run:
22 games (Man. United)

Longest winless run:
15 games (Swindon)

Longest losing run:
7 games (Tottenham)

Highest attendance:
45,347 (Aston Villa v Liverpool)

Lowest attendance:
4,739 (Wimbledon v Coventry)

Average attendance: 23,040

TEAM OF THE **SEASON**

Tim **Flowers**

Gary **Kelly** — Gary **Pallister** — Tony **Adams** — Denis **Irwin**

Paul **Ince** — Gary **McAllister** — David **Batty**

Eric **Cantona** — Alan **Shearer** — Peter **Beardsley**

PFA PLAYER OF THE YEAR:
Eric Cantona (Man. United)

PFA YOUNG PLAYER OF THE YEAR:
Andy Cole (Newcastle)

GOAL OF THE SEASON:
Rod Wallace, 17/04/92
Leeds v Tottenham

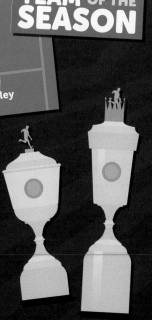

		P	W	D	L	F	A	GD	Pts
1	Man. United	42	27	11	4	80	38	42	92
2	Blackburn	42	25	9	8	63	36	27	84
3	Newcastle	42	23	8	11	82	41	41	77
4	Arsenal	42	18	17	7	53	28	25	71
5	Leeds	42	18	16	8	65	39	26	70
6	Wimbledon	42	18	11	13	56	53	3	65
7	Sheff. Wed.	42	16	16	10	76	54	22	64
8	Liverpool	42	17	9	16	59	55	4	60
9	QPR	42	16	12	14	62	61	1	60
10	Aston Villa	42	15	12	15	46	50	-4	57
11	Coventry	42	14	14	14	43	45	-2	56
12	Norwich	42	12	17	13	65	61	4	53
13	West Ham	42	13	13	16	47	58	-11	52
14	Chelsea	42	13	12	17	49	53	-4	51
15	Tottenham	42	11	12	19	54	59	-5	45
16	Man. City	42	9	18	15	38	49	-11	45
17	Everton	42	12	8	22	42	63	-21	44
18	Southampton	42	12	7	23	49	66	-17	43
19	Ipswich	42	9	16	17	35	58	-23	43
20	Sheff. United	42	8	18	16	42	60	-18	42
21	Oldham	42	9	13	20	42	68	-26	40
22	Swindon	42	5	15	22	47	100	-53	30

1992-93

Manchester United claimed the first ever Premier League title, eventually finishing ten points ahead of second-placed Aston Villa despite the two teams being evenly matched going into April. It also sealed United's first top-flight title for 26 years, and heralded a new era at Old Trafford.

However, the early pace-setters were Norwich, who won ten of their first 16 matches, with Arsenal, Blackburn and Aston Villa close behind. Man. United, who were nine points off the pace in November, signed French striker Eric Cantona from champions Leeds in a move that would have a huge bearing on where the title ended up going.

Blackburn were just three points adrift of the Canaries on Boxing Day but an injury to star striker Alan Shearer hit them hard. The England star, who had scored 16 goals in 21 Premier League games, was ruled out for the rest of the season and Rovers' title ambitions fell away.

Aston Villa's strikeforce of new signing Dean Saunders and Dalian Atkinson terrified Premier League defences, and the Villans were third at the turn of the year. But Man. United's season had gone from strength to strength since losing to Ron Atkinson's side in November, and they edged ahead of Villa on goal difference after 22 matches.

The lead changed hands between the two sides from this point, before United took control on 10 April. They hosted Sheffield Wednesday at Old Trafford and centre-back Steve Bruce scored two late goals, including a 97th-minute winner, as United came from behind to beat the Owls 2-1. On the same day, Aston Villa surrendered top spot after a goalless draw at home to Coventry City.

Alex Ferguson's men stormed to the title from here on. Villa lost their last three matches and Norwich won two of their final six outings, allowing the Red Devils to clinch the title at Old Trafford with a 3-1 win over Blackburn.

At the other end of the table, Nottingham Forest, who bid farewell to retiring manager Brian Clough, finished bottom, while Middlesbrough's relegation was confirmed before the final day of the season. The final relegation place went to the last day of the season. Despite recent wins over Aston Villa and Liverpool, Oldham were still three points from safety going into the final day. But a dramatic 4-3 win over Southampton saw them escape on goal difference at the expense of Crystal Palace, who were relegated after a 3-0 defeat to Arsenal.

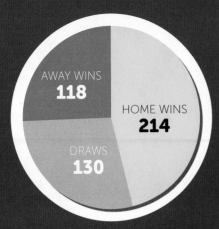

- **AWAY WINS** 118
- **HOME WINS** 214
- **DRAWS** 130

GAMES PLAYED 462
GOALS SCORED 1,222

AVERAGE GOALS/GAME: **2.65**

TOP SCORERS

1. **Teddy Sheringham** — Nottingham Forest/Tottenham — **22**
2. **Les Ferdinand** — Queens Park Rangers — **20**
3. **Dean Holdsworth** — Wimbledon — **19**
4. **Micky Quinn** — Coventry City — **17**
5. **Alan Shearer** — Blackburn Rovers — **16**
6. **David White** — Manchester City — **16**
7. =8 players — **15**

STATS

Biggest transfer:
3.6m Alan Shearer
(Southampton to Blackburn)

Biggest win:
Blackburn 7-1 Norwich

Longest winning run:
7 games (Man. United & Sheff. Wed)

Longest unbeaten run:
11 games (Man. United)

Longest winless run:
13 games (Ipswich)

Longest losing run:
6 games (Nott'm Forest)

Highest attendance:
44,619 (Liverpool v Everton)

Lowest attendance:
3,039 (Wimbledon v Everton)

Average attendance: 21,125

TEAM OF THE SEASON

Peter **Schmeichel**

David **Bardsley** · Gary **Pallister** · Paul **McGrath** · Tony **Dorigo**

Gary **Speed** · Paul **Ince** · Roy **Keane** · Ryan **Giggs**

Alan **Shearer** · Ian **Wright**

PFA PLAYER OF THE YEAR:
Paul McGrath (Aston Villa)

PFA YOUNG PLAYER OF THE YEAR:
Ryan Giggs (Man. United)

GOAL OF THE SEASON:
Dalian Atkinson, 03/10/92
Wimbledon v Aston Villa

		P	W	D	L	F	A	GD	Pts
1	Man. United	42	24	12	6	67	31	36	84
2	Aston Villa	42	21	11	10	57	40	17	74
3	Norwich	42	21	9	12	61	65	-4	72
4	Blackburn	42	20	11	11	68	46	22	71
5	QPR	42	17	12	13	63	55	8	63
6	Liverpool	42	16	11	15	62	55	7	59
7	Sheff. Wed.	42	15	14	13	55	51	4	59
8	Tottenham	42	16	1	15	60	66	-6	59
9	Man. City	42	15	12	15	56	51	5	57
10	Arsenal	42	15	11	16	40	38	2	56
11	Chelsea	42	14	14	14	51	54	-3	56
12	Wimbledon	42	14	12	16	56	55	1	54
13	Everton	42	15	8	19	53	55	-2	53
14	Sheff. United	42	14	10	18	54	53	1	52
15	Coventry	42	13	13	16	52	57	-5	52
16	Ipswich	42	12	16	14	50	55	-5	52
17	Leeds	42	12	15	15	57	62	-5	51
18	Southampton	42	13	11	18	54	61	-7	50
19	Oldham	42	13	10	19	63	74	-11	49
20	Crystal Palace	42	11	16	15	48	61	-13	49
21	Middlesbro	42	11	11	20	54	75	-21	44
22	Nott'm Forest	42	10	10	22	41	62	-21	40